Making Shifts without Making Waves strikes chord with business, health care, church leaders

"Church leaders who take seriously the call to be 'salt and light,' to equip their congregations to transform their communities in the Spirit of Christ, need new approaches to leadership in our rapidly changing times. These authors command a profound grasp of both the 'why' and the 'how.' This book makes an extremely valuable contribution to this critical and timely topic."

Larry Hovis, Executive Coordinator, Cooperative Baptist Fellowship of North Carolina

"In this fast-paced, fast-changing world, leaders are in need of tools and guidelines for managing change and staying focused on the mission of the organization. In this book, Hammett and Pierce have provided just such a tool. The leadership principles outlined here are applicable to a variety of organizations, but I would hope church leaders will pay careful attention and learn well this coaching model. This book is a most helpful resource to equip leaders with skills for asking guiding questions and pointing the way forward in this twenty-first–century world. This 'tool kit' will provide what is necessary for the task ahead, and the soulful leader will discover fresh insights for bold leadership."

Bishop Larry M. Goodpaster, The United Methodist Church,
Western North Carolina Conference

"When congregations and other Christian organizations are ready for transformation, they need a coach approach to soulful leadership for the transitions and changes they must experience. Eddie, Randy, and Steve present a timely and excellent model and very practical tools for making significant shifts. Read, practice, and feel the rush of soulful leadership!"

George Bullard, Ministry Partner, The Columbia Partnership

"Hammett and Pierce offer great insights for anyone involved in helping people, businesses, churches and organizations navigate change. As a missional strategy leader I found the 'coach approach' to change helpful to me as an organizational leader. The practical insights, the excellent coaching tools ,and easy-to-read style make this book a must for any agent of change."

Lonnie Reynolds, International Missional Strategy Leader

"The coach approach is truly a forward-moving process that can help leaders develop the centered focus they need to create change and prevent sabotage. Randy and Eddie have given us an important and challenging work that can provide individuals and systems with the survival tools needed during these fast-moving times. This is a valuable resource."

Patricia Doherty, Nurse Manager, Arbour Health Systems

"Change is coming to every area of our lives. The church is certainly not immune. What is the model for leading a mostly volunteer organization to posture for the coming changes? The authors have designed a most practical and perceptive model for those of us who work in parish ministry. Read this book, but more importantly, put these principles into practice!"

Bo Prosser, Coordinator for Congregational Formation,
National Cooperative Baptist Fellowship

"What's needed today are leaders who move us ahead without wrecking things. As Eddie, Randy and Steve demonstrate, leaders who take a coach approach are ably equipped to do just this. For leaders and organizations who want to realize results and reduce the risks inherent to progress, this is a must read."

Chad Hall, Western Seminary and author of Faith Coaching: A Conversational Approach to Helping Others Move Forward in Faith

MAKING SHIFTS without MAKING WAVES

A Coach Approach to Soulful Leadership

Edward H. Hammett and James R. Pierce
with Stephen DeVane

CHALICE PRESS
ST. LOUIS, MISSOURI

Cover and interior design: Elizabeth Wright

Visit Chalice Press on the World Wide Web at
www.chalicepress.com

10 9 8 7 6 5 4 3 2 1   09   10   11   12   13   14

EPUB: 978-08272-23455 • EPDF: 978-08272-23462

Library of Congress Cataloging-in-Publication Data

Hammett, Edward H.
  Making shifts without making waves : the coach approach to soulful leadership / by Edward H. Hammett, James R. Pierce ; with Stephen DeVane.
      p. cm.
  Includes bibliographical references.
  ISBN 978-0-8272-2337-0
1. Change—Religious aspects. 2. Change—Religious aspects--Christianity. 3. Leadership—Religious aspects. 4. Leadership—Religious aspects—Christianity. 5. Personal coaching. I. Pierce, James R. II. DeVane, Stephen. III. Title.

BL65.C53H36 2009
253—dc22

                                                          2009026757

Printed in United States of America

Contents

Editor's Foreword

Inspiration and Wisdom for Twenty-First-Century Christian Leaders

You have chosen wisely in deciding to study and learn from a book published in **The Columbia Partnership Leadership Series** with Chalice Press. We publish for

- Congregational leaders who desire to serve with greater faithfulness, effectiveness, and innovation.
- Christian ministers who seek to pursue and sustain excellence in ministry service.
- Members of congregations who desire to reach their full kingdom potential.
- Christian leaders who desire to use a coach approach in their ministry.
- Denominational and parachurch leaders who want to come alongside affiliated congregations in a servant leadership role.
- Consultants and coaches who desire to increase their learning concerning the congregations and Christian leaders they serve.

The Columbia Partnership Leadership Series is an inspiration- and wisdom-sharing vehicle of The Columbia Partnership, a community of Christian leaders who are seeking to transform the capacity of the North American Protestant church to pursue and sustain vital Christ-centered ministry. You can connect with us at www.TheColumbiaPartnership.org.

Primarily serving congregations, denominations, educational institutions, leadership development programs, and parachurch organizations, the Partnership also seeks to connect with individuals, businesses, and other organizations seeking a Christ-centered spiritual focus.

We welcome your comments on these books, and we welcome your suggestions for new subject areas and authors we ought to consider.

George W. Bullard Jr., Senior Editor
GBullard@TheColumbiaPartnership.org

The Columbia Partnership,
332 Valley Springs Road, Columbia, SC 29223-6934
Voice: 803.622.0923, www.TheColumbiaPartnership.org

Acknowledgments

A lifetime of learnings and experiences frame the concepts of *Making Shifts without Making Waves: A Coach Approach to Soulful Leadership.* The powerful and life-changing realities of transforming soulful leadership have touched us and challenged us to enter into a transformed life and career that allows us to share these learnings with you.

For all those who have helped us learn, we are indebted. We have worked with organizations in the profit and nonprofit worlds. Churches, businesses, and nonprofit organizations served as our laboratories for over two decades. We have coached teams and organizations of many sizes with a variety of mission statements.

Prior to completing this manuscript, we conducted a learning lab at Hollifield Leadership Center to get feedback and critique. We are deeply indebted to the participants who made this a more practical book.

Steve DeVane has served as our collegue, editor, and ghost writer. He helped us sharpen and focus many of the chapters by offering his refined editorial skills and his perspective. We are deeply grateful for his willingness to collaborate on this project.

Connie Taylor, Chuck McGuire, and Lynn Hartness, fellow spiritual travelers and friends, were among our critics and readers as we wrote. David Tillman also provided valuable feedback. After working with words for months and months on end, words and sentences begin to run together. You need fresh eyes and loving critics. We are deeply grateful for them.

We are also indebted to our families and many colleagues and friends who have been sounding boards, critics, and nurturers of this project. Encouragement and support are often needed while writing a book. We stand blessed.

We are grateful for the encouragement, support, and blessing of our "day jobs"—our friends and colleagues at McGhee Productivity Solutions, Arbour Hospital, and the Baptist State Convention of North Carolina. The Columbia Partnership and Coach Approach Ministries continue to offer nurture of new dreams and fresh visions. We are blessed and grateful for their support.

For the pioneering vision and leadership of The Columbia Partnership leadership series and our publisher, Chalice Press, we will always be grateful. They have made the book strong and continue to offer helpful editing, cover design, and partnership. Our editor at Chalice Press, Trent Butler, continues to sharpen our writings to impact our readers.

Those who gave their endorsement brought their critical eye and years of experience to the reading and evaluating of this manuscript. These professional colleagues represent expertise in a variety of arenas of life. For their willingness to give their endorsements we are deeply grateful.

Finally, without the professional coach training of coaching colleagues, this manuscript content would have never materialized. The wisdom and counsel of Linda Miller (MCC), Jane Creswell (MCC), Suzanne Goebel (PCC), Chad Hall (PCC), and Bill Cooper (ACC) have led us to encounter and embrace many of these powerful discoveries in our lives. Thanks to these soulful leaders who have shared their lives and learnings with us over the last decade.

Preface

The Impact of the Waves of Needed Change

"If you want things to be different, perhaps the answer is to become different yourself."
Norman Vincent Peale

"Change has come to America"

President Barack Obama used that phrase to describe the political reality brought about by his election in November 2008.[1] His description could be applied to nearly every area of life over the past decade.

Baby boomers are aging. A younger generation of leaders thinks about and values different perspectives and issues than their predecessors. It seems that "going green" is at the top of the agenda for many organizations, households, and businesses. Women are stepping into an increasing number of leadership roles in government, education, medicine, science, and economics. Yes, the world is shifting.

In these and other ways, most profit and nonprofit organizations, businesses, families, employees, churches, and denominations are experiencing exponential waves of change creating shifts of focus, energies, resources, and/or personnel. Technology continues to impact us all, from iPhones to iPods to computers of every size and shape and function. Now we are even seeing hints of holographic technology. An increasing number of meetings are being held online. Such new waves create new challenges that move us to a greater need for efficiency, effectiveness, and timeliness. On-demand learning and steep learning curves face every person, institution, business, and organization.

Making Shifts without Making Waves: A Coach Approach to Soulful Leadership recognizes that these historic shifts will create waves that challenge and waves that create new opportunities. The waves are certain to call for shifts in the way we view things and accomplish objectives. Regardless of whether you are churched or unchurched; Anglo, African American, Hispanic, Italian, Indian, Korean, Asian, or Latino; rich or poor; Republican, independent, or Democrat—change is here. We will all continue to be touched in one way or another over the next decades. This is the reality we face as families, businesses, churches, nonprofit organizations, government agencies, schools, and communities.

We believe a soulful leader is a person who desires and is equipped for *transforming influence and has transformational impact*. As a result of such leadership, people, organizations, families, and businesses successfully encounter waves and experience shifts. We further believe that *transformational impact* can only occur after tough decisions are made and attitudes and behaviors are *changed*. These changes lead to the *transitional steps* in individuals and organizations that yield revolutionary transformation.

Revolutionary Transformation = Change + Transition.

In this book we will be introducing a toolkit that will generate transformation: a new ripple model, seven key questions that make shifts without making waves, basics of coaching, and how to move through BARRIERS and create BRIDGES.

Postmodern Shifts and Their Influence

The realities of today's and tomorrow's culture include a graying and a secularization of America. Our demographics are shifting from white Anglo Saxon Protestants toward people of color. The poor and the wealthy segments of the population are increasing, while the middle class seems to be disappearing. In 2008–2009, the financial industry experienced a meltdown, the price of oil skyrocketed, and families and businesses experienced overwhelming challenges. Health concerns, educational challenges, and relational and family issues abound in every community.

Fewer and fewer are honoring the sacred vows of marriage. Family life is becoming more and more based on relationships rather than blood, legal, or religious commitments. Interracial and multicultural relationships are growing, creating challenges and difficulties for some. The world also faces what some see as "global warming," while others deny its reality and influence. Diversity of opinions and alignments are prevalent so every family, organization, institution, church, and government faces many waves of change and challenge. These will call for shifts that some will embrace easily and others will resist. Obama's election, along with many other new realities, calls forth the best in us if we are to move forward rather than get trapped in blame games or hostilities. *Making Shifts without Making Waves* provides tools, coaching models, and insights for leaders and organizations that will strengthen our unity around issues of hope, healing, health, and desires to be better, not bitter.

The election and the other new cultural and educational realities represent a seismic shift in our country. We now have an opportunity to move forward, but new skills are required. Challenging external realities are calling forth internal shifts that can propel leaders and organizations to flourish in this time of change and challenge. Otherwise, they will simply build fortresses and barriers that threaten the very fabric of who we are and who we desire to become.

During this election campaign, the Internet, for the first time, proved to be a significant force in raising funds for political purposes and in engaging the younger generation in a political movement. Worldwide formal and informal dialogues, blogs, and online forums shaped and reshaped our political and cultural landscape in ways that will be felt for at least the next decade.

The stress and challenge of transformation is everywhere. It gives us a powerful gift and an opportunity to build bridges instead of barriers with other ethnic groups, economic realities, relational challenges, and faith perspectives. History is clear that change creates challenge. It also generates opportunity and momentum when persons decide to move forward. This is the hope, message, and toolkit *Making Shifts without Making Waves* offers to you.

Ken Blanchard, internationally respected author of the bestseller *The One Minute Manager* and countless other books, recently co-authored with Phil Hodges a modern-day parable for the church—*The Most Loving Place in Town*. The book is a narrative of a pastor and congregation who are faced with change and the fears and apprehensions that often go with any change. In this book they summarize concepts of the "soulful leader" and powerful learnings about implementing change.

- All lasting change starts with clear vision and direction.
- The first thing people want to know when faced with change is information.
- The next thing they have are personal concerns—they want to know how the change will affect them.
- Once people's personal concerns are dealt with, they want to know what the implementation plans are—what will happen first, second, third, and so on.
- After these questions have been dealt with, people are more open to hear about the benefits of the change.
- When implementing change, you don't have to do it all on your own.
- Developing a strategy to deal with fear and pride issues is important in any change effort.[2]

Another perspective regarding a soulful leader and change comes from a colleague and friend and is worth considering. John Trent writes about *HeartShifts* and the importance and power of making "two-degree shifts" in behaviors, thinking, or maybe values, to make meaningful and transforming change. He challenges us to work from our strengths rather than our weaknesses and to be intentional about making meaningful heart shifts. We agree. We affirm his beliefs about building "memorial markers" to celebrate the days you make heart shifts.[3] Such insights are key in helping leaders and organizations make shifts without making overwhelming waves.

The Impact and Influence of Soulful Leaders

Consider your organization, your leadership style, your value system, and your dreams and desires. How can you be effective, successful, and all that God intends you to be in this day of change and challenge? That is the focus of *Making Shifts without Making Waves: A Coach Approach to Soulful Leadership*. Our book offers a coach approach to introducing and managing change and provides tools for the making of a soulful leader and soulful organization. The models, tools, skills, and encouragement we offer will help you face change with courage, hope, health, and clarity.

You will note that throughout the book special graphic markings lead you to specific kinds of materials. *Coaching questions are bulleted lists bounded by bracketed boxes. Reflective questions for the coach have a line above and below each set of questions. Teaching boxes are shaded for your quick reference.* We are also providing more than normal white space in our writings so that this might truly be a handbook that you will use in many aspects of your lives. You will want to make notes of your learnings and powerful connections that this coach approach empowers you to make. This will allow you to build ownership of the next steps for your family, organization, faith group, or yourself as a leader. The challenge we now face is how to become soulful leaders of soulful organizations that generate transforming influence and impact because of who we are and what our destinies hold.

Edward (Eddie) H. Hammett,
James R. (Randy) Pierce,
with Stephen (Steve) DeVane
October 2009

Introduction

Critical Times Call for Soulful Leadership

Very often people find themselves facing storms—hurricanes, tornados, droughts, heat waves, hail, or fierce rains. People also face other types of storm—and so do secular, religious, profit, and nonprofit organizations of all types and sizes. These storms often involve one or more of the following:

- Shifting demographics that begin to impact client base or membership
- Diminishing funding for effective programming, ministries, or services
- Decline in interest, revenue, or support for one reason or another
- Decline in impact and effectiveness
- Decrease in leadership base and loss of talent
- Chaos created by dysfunctional, compulsive, or addictive behaviors
- Stress created by mismatch of calling and placement in a career, place of ministry, or service
- Stress generated when we are called to deal with differences—of ethnicity, lifestyle, generations, culture, traditions, values, etc
- Poor focus and no direction

This book provides practical tools that have proven to help persons, organizations, churches, families, judicatories, and denominations weather these storms and others. It's not an easy task, but the proven toolkit found here will offer guidance in those times when the rains and storm clouds diminish sight and escalate fears. These storms of change are around every corner these days.

Today's changing world makes many people uncomfortable. Consider these examples:

- *Businesses* compete for new ideas, productive products, and an efficient workforce. They're forced to do more with less in a shaky economy.
- *Families* experience an increasing number of pressures. Diverse family relationships, economic challenges, fast-paced lives, and stressors are around most corners, making it difficult for families to maintain balance.
- *Schools* seek more efficient, cost-effective ways of educating the existing and future generations. Learning styles are more varied than ever.
- *Churches* experience generational distinctives and a host of personal preferences of worship styles, learning styles, and values concerning the role of spiritual formation in life. Denominational loyalty rapidly declines, while new networks of mission activity and support grow.
- *Other nonprofit and mission-driven companies* struggle with volunteer enlistment, creative fund raising and sponsorships, and doing more with less.

Amidst all this, change and transition are consistent threads. To move forward inevitably requires adjusting to change, which always calls for courage. New disciplines, higher awareness, spiritual discernment, and new learning styles are needed to activate that courage. Leaders struggle with how to deal with overwhelming newness driven by technological advances, economic shifts, and generational differences. Most leaders want to keep their current clients or members happy, fearing a loss of support from overchallenging them. Churches and other organizations realize they must attract and learn to serve effectively the younger generations if they are to maintain their customer or membership base in the future.

The issue then becomes, for all, how do you make needed shifts without making too many waves? How do you move an organization, family, business, church, or denomination from just maintenance values to those of forward movement and mission? This question is partially fueling the growing movement of spirituality in the workplace. Companies and leaders of companies are seeking ways to recapture integrity and balance in life and work. In *Megatrends 2010*, the author lists seven megatrends—two of which are specific to spirituality in the business world: (1) The Power of Spirituality and (4) Spirituality in Business. The other five trends relate to values, influence, and moral authority.[1] How does a business face the challenge of facing such trends and incorporating a response to them in the organization's basic identity? Coaching offers one significant aid in meeting this challenge.

The coach approach offers committed soulful leaders and organizations a skill set and perspective based on discernment, hope, future progress, and actions that are decided and made through consensus and ownership of a next step. This collaborative approach can help soulful leaders discover the organization's soul and its potential in an ever-changing environment. Thinking a group can thrive amidst change and create no waves is unrealistic. In similar fashion, not every person, group, or organization is best led by or open to the coach approach. Still, with the coach approach, a group of most any kind can certainly build ownership of a new vision and make plans to enter that destiny with deep commitment. How possible is it? It is possible and probable.

The chart on page xiv can guide you, with the help of a good coach, to do some valuable self-assessment when it comes to probable shifts needed in determining awareness and readiness in making some of these shifts for the organization's progress. This New Communication Manifesto[2] frames "what's in" and "what's out" for persons in or working to communicate with the digital generation (generally speaking those persons forty years of age and under).

- What are your thoughts when you review this chart?
- What three issues do you feel need to be considered seriously to increase your effectiveness as an individual or organization?
- What do you need to do to make these shifts?

We are keenly aware that this book promises much in the title. Our experience over the last decade of leadership in various organizations proves the power and practicality of concepts we are introducing to you here. Throughout the book you will find a sampling of powerful coaching questions. We will also be suggesting some reflective questions for your consideration. These are keys to helping leaders and organizations make internal shifts so external and organizational shifts can happen with only predictable ripples of change, not destructive waves of change.

We suspect that many readers will find the chart's list more than overwhelming, if not confusing and frustrating. Some will say, "I like things the way they are—why are these shifts needed?" Others will say, "The author of this chart 'gets it,' and we need to pay attention!" Such reactions simply illustrate the diversity of views and values in most organizations.

Our hope is that as you read this book you might think of a pebble being thrown into a pond where *ripples move from the inside to the outside*. This image expresses how a soulful leader who possesses good coaching and leadership skills can move from a dictated approach to change that usually makes waves to a collaborative approach that may have ripples, but not overwhelming waves. That is the focus of this book and the drive that brought your authors to share, from our experience, practical and proven coaching steps of introducing and managing change that leads to transformation without destroying your organization or your spirit.

The New Communication Manifesto for the Digital Generation

WHAT'S OUT	WHAT'S IN
Legacy dogmas	New realities
Watching, reading, and listening	Doing, simulating, and engaging
Telling	Conversation and application
Sage-on-a-stage	Ubiquitous training
Command and control	Guide and nurture
Top-down	Peer-to-peer
Father knows best	Harnessing collective intelligence
Plan and execute	Release early and often, perpetual beta
Cautious and safe	Wacky and rebellious
Ask for permission	Ask for forgiveness
People going to training	Training going to people
Interruptive distractions	Teachable moments
Appointment-driven	On-demand
Captives in meetings	Communications in context
Graphic design	Game design
Efficiency and cost control	Effectiveness and growth
Replicating communications with new media	Reinventing communications with new media
Compliance	Commitment

SECTION
ONE

The Impact of
Soulful Leadership

Making Shifts without Making Waves

Is It Really Possible?

Change creates a storm crashing on the shorelines of our time.

A small business increases sales and profits by 50 percent, but cannot get an extension of its credit line at the bank. In fact, the bank wants to reduce the line of credit by half. Will the waves of insufficient capital drown the growing business?

A fighting family finds peace in a new city and a new church. Then a new peer group forms for the children, leading them to resent and rebel against their stepfather and his and their mother's new faith. Will the waves of anger and resentment destroy what appeared to be a growing relationship of love and respect?

A successful businessman suddenly realizes life has lost any meaning it ever had. What can this man, filled with pain and lacking a clear purpose, do? How does a person get untangled from the bondage of addictive and dysfunctional behaviors that continue to rob him of freedom, healthy relationships, and fulfillment of his destiny?

A growing, strong, traditional church changes pastors and leadership. Quarrels develop between the pastor and the music minister. The rousing hymnal and anthem music had been the talk of the town, drawing new members from all around and filling the auditorium for special music programs. Suddenly, the same programs fail to attract people. The crowds swarm the new independent church down the road with its huge screens, contemporary music, movie clips, and loud praise band. Waves

> Postmodernity is most often a mind-set and attitude that is not just representative of an age group.

1

are beginning to roar in the traditional church. What can they do to make shifts in their programs and goals without drowning in the waves of newness?

Most of us can extend this list of examples from business, church, personal, or school life. Too often we find ourselves seemingly overwhelmed by life's storms.

Just as a powerful hurricane levels anything else in its path, postmodernity, the global economy, diversity in the workplace, changing family structures, and other issues are laying flat traditional thinking. This is not simply a brief squall that is passing over. Postmodernism and these other factors are growing rapidly and gathering hurricane force. Postmodernity is most often a mind-set and attitude not just representative of an age group. Leonard Sweet outlines postmodernity's most prevalent shifts:

- propositional to experiential connections to truth
- individualistic to communal experiences
- theoretical to authentic values
- naïve certainty to a deeper understanding of struggle[1]

Waves of change sometimes present a choice to make. You can accept the change and align yourself to it (e.g., it's cold or rainy and you decide to wear a coat and take an umbrella), or you can reject or ignore the change and venture into the storm unprotected and unprepared. Other times change presents itself in pressing waves that just do not subside. Then you have to deal with a new reality in one way or the other (for example, the circumstances surrounding the 9–11 attacks creating a "new norm"; North America's shift from agrarian culture to industrial; information technology's progress from Gutenberg's printing press to computers you can hold in your hand). People and organizations eventually feel the pinch of those waves of change that do not subside. The intensity of the pinch and its consequences bring people and organizations to the point of having to make changes (for example, an organization finally surrenders its written memos and printing press for computers, e-mail, video-conferencing, etc.). Pain and constant discomfort (especially on the bottom line) often create an openness to change that otherwise would not have happened.

Sweet points out that people operating from a postmodern perspective have a loss of confidence in both premodern authority figures and modern reason. For postmoderns, he said, it is less "Aha! Now I get it. I've figured it out" and more "Aha! Now I feel it. I've experienced exactly what you're talking about."[2] Added to the philosophical changes are major reality shifts. As of this writing, a sinking mortgage industry is creating ripples throughout the economy, family systems, educational systems, retail, and the oil industry. The pinch is on.

> **Pain and constant discomfort often create an openness to change that otherwise would not have existed.**

> **Methods that worked ten, five, even two years ago are hopelessly out of date.**

Change Creates Storms

Some ripples are inevitable, but a variety of keys, strategies, and a conscious leadership style can lead you and your organization in making shifts without making waves. Sweet accurately calls the current environment "one of the greatest culture storms ever."[3] In a review of Sweet's book on Amazon.com, George Bullard notes that organizations should prepare in ways metaphorically similar to those ships use when getting ready for a hurricane. Ships head out to sea to maneuver around the storm.

Many leaders today understand the forecast and recognize change as it makes landfall. Yet, knowledge itself is an inadequate instrument for navigating in the storm. Tools leaders once used to deal with incremental change no longer fit the massive shifts of today. Methods that worked ten, five, even two years ago are hopelessly out of date to deal with the exponential changes of our day. In this rapid-paced culture of change, a leader trained to manage is not enough. Serious and challenging times call for a soulful leader.

Serious and challenging times call for a soulful leader.

- Soulful leaders trust their heart, intuition, and curiosity as well as their knowledge—they integrate head and heart into leadership.
- Soulful leaders push through their fears.
- Soulful leaders understand the value of moving beyond their comfort zones.
- Soulful leaders honor other people and value their ideas during the process of change.
- Soulful leaders work to lead by consensus when possible, believing collaboration is more important than dictating mandates.
- Soulful leaders trust methods but also trust their soul's voice as they use methods.
- Soulful leaders know the bottom line is important in leadership of any organization.
- Soulful leaders value the divine alignments of their values and beliefs as well as how they live them out in times of change and challenge.
- Soulful leaders value integrity and accountability.
- Soulful leaders take action.
- Soulful leaders take risks.
- Soulful leaders are strategic.
- Soulful leaders develop a skill set to transform.

Soulful leaders push through their fears.

Do you practice leadership by the book, or do you follow your soul in making decisions? Patricia Aburdene reminds us, "As individuals grow in consciousness and Spirit, so do the organizations they inhabit." She further clarifies:

The problem is organizations take longer to change than people do. Why is institutional change more difficult? Because it is so complex. Not only does it require time, vision and leadership, it involves a greater number of people, their commitment and the development of a shared purpose. Institutional transformation relies on human evolution that grows slowly, then finally hits the mark.[4]

Even worse, often old tools and outdated methods cause more problems than they solve. It is becoming more and more challenging for leaders to lead their businesses or organizations and also remain students, themselves. Yet soulful leaders must acquire deeper learnings to sharpen their own skills and to stay abreast of all the constant changes. Cultural and global challenges abound, providing new horizons for most leaders and organizations. Walking into these waves without getting wiped out or consumed by rip tides is a skill. Learning to read the waves and time behaviors allows one to ride the waves, making the shifts that are needed. Leadership is critical, but the right leadership skills are even more critical, regardless of the organization you are in or are leading. The age of change makes it increasingly important for leaders not to just do things right but to do the right things for the new emerging world.

Soulful leaders take risks.

Do you follow your soul in making decisions?

A New Perspective for New Challenges

Many leaders and organizations would like to avoid change, ignore the need, or deny the pressing realities and shifts around them. In fact, many have been and remain in denial. That is why so many organizations and leaders have become irrelevant in the postmodern world. In the increasingly rapid change of this postmodern age, denial or avoidance is no longer an option. The waves are here; the need for shifts are paramount. Now we must face it—we're in the storm. We can let it destroy us, or we can learn to ride the waves of healthy change and transition.

A new approach is needed to help today's leaders make shifts without making waves that destroy. One such approach can be found in the profession of coaching. The coach approach has helped leaders focus their lives and find their purpose. The coach approach can help those same leaders manage their organizations through change. Such change brings gale force uncertainty and surging uneasiness. A coach approach lets leaders put their organizational ships out to sea to maneuver in the storm, knowing that high winds and storm surges will damage any vessel moored in the port of predictability and the harbor of habit. Allowing flexibility of movement and openness of pliability is needed for healthy productive change.

Leaders using the coach approach help their organizations to not only weather the storm, but also to meet the challenge of making shifts without causing further destructive waves. Coaching allows the waves to subside to ripples that gradually allow the individual and/or the organization to embrace and create change. This is the beginning step to transformation.

One Person Can Make a Difference!

So often in the emotions that surround change, tempers flare, personal conflicts emerge, and relationships dissolve amidst differing personal agendas and efforts to "be right." One powerful question often can "bottom line" the issue: "Do we want to be right, or do we want the relationship?" Notice, as Eddie shares two powerful personal experiences, how much power one person can have when seeking to make shifts without making waves.

One of the most powerful pieces in the *Reaching People Under 40 While Keeping People Over 60* book is my "grandmother story." During my college years, my home church invited me to serve as a part-time staff person. I was assigned the responsibility of moving my grandmother's Sunday school class. This sounded simple enough to me, since the fire marshal had declared that new rules required that our baby nursery be moved closer to an outside exit. My grandmother's class was near an exit, their room was much more spacious, and their membership was declining. Another factor assured me of the ease of this assignment. Most of the ladies in her class had diapered me in the nursery during my toddler years.

Suffice it to say that the idea, though practical and "required by the fire marshal" was not readily accepted by the Sunday school class. They had been in that room for several decades and had made it "their own." My grandmother was not happy either. So much so that she closed the door on our regular Sunday lunches at her house. She also declared that she and I would pray and dialogue to discover what could be done—now that I had "torn up her Sunday school class." Her wisdom guided our relationship for the next painful months. She eventually discovered, and declared to me and to her peers, "I have come to understand that my [our] personal comfort is not as important as this church's mission." After she revealed this new conviction to her fellow classmates, they picked up their chairs and moved to a small room, creating space in their old room for a nursery that was growing. We never heard another complaint from them, *and* they became engaged in ministering to the newborns and their families.

Another personal illustration happened during the days when I (Eddie) was battling heart trouble and facing open-heart surgery. My family's expectation was always that our pastor, or the pastors of family members who went to other churches,

The coach approach has helped leaders focus their lives and find their purpose.

One person can make a difference!

were to come and pray for those in our family who were about to undergo surgery. I felt that this was no longer a wise expectation or need—our family could pray! So I called each pastor and asked them not to come to my bedside prior to surgery. After all, it was 5 a.m. in the morning. Our family and friends were present at my bedside that morning. Each began to ask," Where's my pastor?" I revealed that I had asked them not to come. They seemed to understand my logic and wish. The next moments were some I would not trade for anything. I heard and observed our family make some very needed shifts in their pastoral expectations as we experienced some of the most powerful prayer times our family has ever shared together! Now our family no longer has the pastoral expectation assumption—in fact, now we celebrate where we can beat the pastor to a bedside and pray ourselves.

Granted, I was not utilizing all of the powerful coaching skills in full in these scenarios. I was using principles and questions we share here. The impact was transformational change of internal beliefs that impacted external behaviors and ultimately influenced and impacted others without creating tidal waves of emotions around emotionally volatile issues.

Most leaders want to make shifts without making waves. They don't want to hurt people or make people mad in the midst of change and transition, but it is often unavoidable. Sometimes Grandma must hurt and stew before change can come. Sometimes family must experience the new before they can ignore the old. Leaders who constantly walk this tightrope can find in the coach approach principles, concepts, and insights to minimize personal and organizational trauma. The result will be significant change that insures growth and progress.

An example that might relate to more of you might be Nick Vujicic (www.lifewithoutlimbs.org or www.attitudeisaltitude. com) moving from life without limbs to life without limits. Nick was born without arms or legs, but the love he holds overcomes any physical limitations. We encourage you to take the time to view his Web sites and transformational videos.

> Personal comfort is not as important as this church's mission.

Soulful Leadership
Creates Transformation
through Coaching

Coaching tools can be used in most any organization. One group that serves as a prime example of their effectiveness is the church.

Richard Florida says most current institutions value things that turn away and discredit, rather than nurture and cultivate, those persons in what he calls the "Creative Class," the innovators of our day.[1] Nowhere is that more evident today than the church and her failing organizations. Churches are barely weathering the culture storm of change as leaders often make more waves than they do shifts. The church has refused to lift anchor as the storm hits, becoming a drag for many church people and effectively turning off the unchurched.

Coaching tools can be used in any organization.

What's the problem? In a culture in which spiritual thirst is at an all time high and many are searching for meaning to life's challenges, why are many churched persons dropping out of church, and why are many spiritual travelers not finding the church a help in their spiritual journey?

Here are some of the things the church's own members say:

- "My church spends more time debating trivial issues (that we make big) than we spend discipling those who are spiritually hungry."
- "Why do many church people focus on preserving tradition rather than finding ways to penetrate the contemporary world with the Good News?"

- "I'm tired of fighting with church people about issues that those in the world we are supposed to be trying to reach find irrelevant."
- "My church refuses to rethink the way we do church and make it more relevant and convenient for my busy family. I have no choice but to drop out."

Other church members complain that the church has become miserable because things have changed. They say the church no longer pleases them or meets their needs. Still other church members say they have become dissatisfied with church when people unlike them started attending.

The unchurched are straightforward about their views. "Church people are more concerned about church that pleases them than church that is meaningful to me," one said. The business world echoes a pervasive cry for honesty, authenticity, integrity, and work that is meaningful. Authors such as Ken Blanchard, Patrick Lencioni, Jane Creswell, John Trent, Linda Miller, Sally McGhee, and John Maxwell address these and other principles in the business world. (See appendices for additional resources.)

The church has refused to lift anchor as the storm hits, becoming a drag for many church people and effectively turning off the unchurched.

Storms prune and purify.

"Christians embrace the wind. And pass out kites."[3]

The Church in the Storm

Leonard Sweet notes that Christians are heading "into one of the greatest culture storms ever,"[2] and follows by explaining something of the value and history of storms for the church. According to Sweet, the church (and most organizations in our 2010+ world) are facing three category five storms—all overlapping, mutually reinforcing storms to create collectively what Sweet notes might be called the "perfect storm."

1. Tsunami known as postmodernity
2. The Big Hurricane, or more precisely an epidemic of related hurricanes, called post-Christendom
3. Global warming[4]

Hope remains for those tossed about in these storms of our time. Sweet recalls, "In both the book and the movie *The Perfect Storm*, there was one reason to go out into the storm and risk being lost at sea: to make the ultimate catch." Sweet argues, and we agree, that the perfect storm offers the church its greatest chance to become the "Ultimate Church" and make the ultimate catch for the gospel. (Similarly, companies have the opportunity to become the "Ultimate Company.") If churches can navigate this sea of change and cross this ranging "Red Sea," we will find a promised land of new beginnings and new church on the other side. Churches can know for certain that the future will be far better for the church than was the past. However, many churches (organizations/businesses) will be left behind, smashed on the shoals of status-quoism, or sink into oblivion.

Storms prune and purify. They tear down all that is not tied down and lasting. They enforce the rule of persevere or perish. It behooves us to make the most of our storms. Colin Morris, a British Methodist, reminds us, "God wills a new creation which may be a gift from beyond history, the kingdom of heaven, but which is made up of elements from every era in history that have withstood the shaking, gone through the refiner's fire and had the dross burned off them."[5]

"When everyone and everything is spinning and whirling in the wind, Christians go out to meet the storm. Christians embrace the wind. And pass out kites."[6]

Whether we represent a church, a nonprofit group, a business, a family, or a community, storms loom in our future. They can tip your boat over, or they can offer great, new, challenging opportunities to move forward, develop new skills, new products, new ways of delivery, and maybe even new clients, members, or colleagues.[7]

Shifts happen. Some are planned, while others are unintentional.

What are you willing to learn from the storms or shifts life brings your way? How open are you to learning and facing steep learning curves with faith, courage, and hope? Write your thoughts below:

The coach approach is a powerful leadership tool that honors the best in humans.

Shifts happen. Some are planned while others unintentional. Some shifts are internal. They might be linked to self-image, openness to the Spirit, addictions, or belief systems. Others are external. They can occur after terrorist attacks, economic downturns, death, health problems, business partners' new policies, or family challenges. Before learning to handle shifts without making waves, leaders must first acquire skills to make smooth the often-turbulent journey. The coach approach offers such skills.

Attunement is not always a viable option for the decision maker or employee when change comes.

Attunement or Alignment?

A coach approach is a powerful leadership tool that honors the best in humans and believes that answers to life, career, economic, family, and relational challenges are found within as clarity is gained through healthy reflection, exploration, and discernment.

Coaching is a brain-altering experience.

• Ask, don't tell.
• Listen, don't talk.
• Rethink your value.
• Understand that your reactions reveal your worldview.[9]

The coach approach is as concerned about attunement as it is alignment. Alignment is often about control and is usually forced. Attunement is more about seeing the value in the tough decisions needing to be made, building consensus, and adjusting out of desire to be "in tune" with others and with the objectives being proposed. Attunement is not always a viable option for the decision maker or employee when change comes.

Coaching and soulful leadership can explore the viability of attunement and make change and transitions more a work of transformation of heart and structure. Discovering and discerning these answers is the power of coaching as it connects the mind, heart, and spirit. Jane Creswell explains, "Coaching is a brain-altering experience. The new insights you'll help people gain through your coaching creates new synapses and neural pathways in their brains and it's a brain-altering experience for you the coach as well. In order to coach others, you'll first have to clarify and adjust your assumptions about people."[8]

Shifts that the coach approach calls for and helps a soulful leader make include:

> • Ask, don't tell.
> • Listen, don't talk.
> • Rethink your value.
> • Understand that your reactions reveal your worldview.[10]

The "person being coached" (PBC) is responsible for his or her own learnings. Coaching is about helping people take responsibility for their lives and decisions. Coaches are guided by a differing set of skills and values than most other consultants or facilitators. Coaching is distinctive in a variety of ways.

One such coaching skill is discernment—the ability to forecast approaching storms, to understand the existing environment, to read the oncoming waves. In short, the leader must recognize and understand the current reality. "Coaching," says Creswell, "is a positive approach that looks to the future. It is an accountability process that helps the person being coached set goals, find solutions, and make forward progress."[11]

This approach can also be applied to groups. Coaching is not about telling or directing. Powerful questions can help the leader see the organization clearly enough to move the group forward toward its goals.

A Metaphor for Coaching

In the following account, Randy (James) relates how he was reminded of coaching's impact during a recent trip.

As I was arriving at the airport, I found myself once again in the long line going through security. I love watching people. It serves as a great coping skill while waiting for long lines to move. As I watched, more and more people became frustrated and agitated with the gridlock. People were taking laptops out of bags, slipping off shoes and belts, and checking each pocket twice. They placed their belongings in trays for the x-ray machines and then walked through the metal detectors. As the line began to move, I immediately observed the next person in line beginning to relax a bit as they took their appropriate action of the next steps to move them forward.

I simply grinned as I thought how similar it was to the affects of good coaching: taking action and moving forward. No one likes to feel stuck or—even worse—move backward. Coaching is all about putting your thoughts, ideas, and passions into action to get to the next step.

The person being coached (PBC) is responsible for his or her own learnings.

After making it through the security line, people want to quickly get to the next step—arrive at the gate; perhaps grab a paper, a quick beverage, or a bite to eat; and make a last bathroom stop before boarding the plane. Then in line to board the plane, the process starts again. Most people want to quickly board and get settled, some being the first to claim an overhead spot for carry-on luggage, coats, and laptops. I observe again how people know where they want to go, but wait for interference to get out of the way. In our lives we sometimes need to move our own interference, but in this scenario I would not recommend it. I don't think the person in front of you would be very happy if you executed a "block and tackle" move to simply get ahead in the boarding line! Once again, I observe more satisfaction as everyone participates in the next steps of movement.

Coaching is not about telling or directing.

On the plane, I notice everyone's need and longing to stay connected. Many send their last text, e-mail, or phone call before the announcement from the airline attendant to turn off all electronic devices. It almost never fails—someone on the plane needs two or three reminders and a stern look from the attendant to "wrap it up" and turn the device off. You assume the attendant is wondering, "Why is there always one on every flight?"

Coaching opens the process for self-discovery and a confidential relationship.

So, everyone is seated and thinks the plane is ready to take off. As we are sitting on the tarmac, the pilot announces that we are tenth in line. I immediately felt the energy shift on the plane as I heard sighs and soft moans. Once the plane begins to move, a feeling of progress, of movement forward to where we all want to be, engulfs the travelers. If you truly stop and allow yourself to observe this next time you are traveling, you can honestly feel the shifts in the energy on the plane.

This is how coaching works. Coaching opens the process for self-discovery and a confidential relationship. It helps an individual or organization connect the dots for movement forward, unleashing potential to move interference out of the way and make things happen quickly.

The plane lands at our destination. As soon as the wheels hit the runway, many reach to turn on their wireless devices. "What e-mails, texts, and voicemails have I missed?" We all rush to be connected again, to gather the data we need for our own next steps. Moving forward and staying connected are two main ingredients necessary for effective coaching.

Finding the Focus and Keeping It

A coach's most challenging function with an individual or group is to help the client find focus and keep it. In a busy world with so much stimuli and information, it is increasingly difficult for persons or organizations to focus enough to make decisions and move forward. In fact, focus is often the major issue that compels an organization to get a coach. Facilitators and consultants bring in more information. Coaches take the information the group already has and help focus it in ways that allow them to frame and work on their agenda for forward movement.

Focus is achieved through skillful listening and asking powerful questions along with tracking of the information being shared. Some focusing questions might include:

- What would you like to talk about today?
- What would be most helpful to talk about now?
- Which piece of what you shared is most critical now?
- How would you prioritize the importance of those things you would like to discuss?
- Which of the top three would you like to resolve now?

Maintaining focus is another challenge. The coach has to listen carefully for disconnects with the focused agenda when detours emerge. The coach has to determine if the information being shared is fruitful for the focused agenda or if it's a personal agenda or a story that has little or no significance in moving forward. Then this observation needs to be checked with the group as a whole. The coach can make a decision, but it's best if this decision is embraced and made by a consensus of the group being coached.

Moving forward and staying connected are two main ingredients necessary for effective coaching.

A coach's challenge is finding the focus and keeping it.

Focus is achieved through skillful listening and asking powerful questions.

Soulful Leaders Create Harmony through Coaching

Change with integrity seems to be the cry of the day. Some want it; others resist it. Some seek to make it happen; still others are tossed and turned because of it. We find it in politics, government, education, businesses, families, communities, economics, congregations, and denominations. Since change seems to be everywhere these days, the challenge is to learn to create harmony without making too many waves or causing too much chaos.

Waves are inevitable in most climates and circumstances. Sometimes the waves bring energy that moves things that have been stationary for too long. Other times the waves bring great force that destroys treasured possessions and dreams. At times we have the option of making waves that matter. Influencing the power of change is possible. People in times of hurricanes fill sandbags to redirect waves and to withstand waves, which sometimes prevents what seems like inevitable destruction. Similar possibilities exist for intentional leaders in organizations to change by utilizing the coach approach. Obviously, in emergency circumstances quick confrontation may be needed, not coaching. If we could have the best of circumstances when change is called for, coaching offers powerful tools (as described later) for making shifts without making—unnecessary or overwhelming—waves. Moving toward harmony and attunement or from maintenance to mission are often desired outcomes for families, organizations, churches, or teams when difficulties known as "pinches" enter the picture.

Change with integrity seems to be the cry of the day.

Coaching is about creating space so the transformation can happen.

Soulful leaders engage others.

13

For this reason, *coaching is a profession and skill set whose time has come*. People, businesses, and churches are searching for ways to save time, energy, and resources while at the same time moving forward and making adjustments in light of new knowledge and challenges. *Coaches are confidential companions* who move people and organizations from where they are to where they want to be. *Coaching is about creating sacred space so that transformation can happen*. Working with an individual or group, a *coach co-creates transformation* in an environment that is safe but challenging. This chapter speaks of the many shifts and skills—some internal and some external—needed by *leaders and organizations to establish a coaching culture* that will enable healthy and effective change, rather than change that is disconcerting and painful.

The soulful leader empowers and encourages.

Creating a Coaching Culture Facilitates Effective Transformation

No leader wants to create tension or dissention in his/her organization when change is needed. Dictatorial leaders simply announce change and demand that others align themselves with it—or else. *Laissez-faire* leaders see the need and desire change, but are such people pleasers and dislike conflict so much that they often avoid change and frequently sabotage the potential in the organization. Soulful leaders see the need for transformation and know that, in order for others to buy into the shifts needed for the organization to flourish, others need to have a voice in the change and transition so they understand the need. Soulful leaders engage others from the very beginning in evaluating the need for change, inviting them into the dialogue and giving them a voice in the plans as they are crafted. The soulful leader empowers and encourages others to help implement the group's visions and decisions.

Four powerful coaching questions:

- What's working?
- What's not working?
- What will make it better?
- Who can champion the change needed now?

What needs to happen when using the coach approach for introducing and managing change? The coach approach is not top down commands for change, but rather involves inviting others into the transformation process. Coaches hear what others think and consider what they feel needs to change. Coaches lead the group to assess needs, decide the sequence for change, build ownership, and evaluate the effectiveness of change. *Creating a coaching culture* in an organization might be summarized best in four powerful coaching questions:

- What's working?
- What's not working?
- What will make it better?
- Who can champion the change needed now?

Facing the Challenge of the Coach Approach

Creating a coaching culture in an organization is worthy of another book in itself. Meanwhile, here are some pointers for working with an organization that seems coachable.

Creating a coaching culture takes time. You begin with key people who are most coachable and interested in moving forward. Building such an atmosphere often requires a contract or covenant between those who show the most enthusiasm for change. They are enlisted to serve as internal coaches and become the first round of coach trainees, who model for others the skill and impact of the coach approach.

Creating a coaching culture begins with the leadership, openness, and coachability of the organization or group involved. The soulful leader is called to coach, not be a directive leader.

Soulful leaders learn new skills and embrace their value in creating organizational advancements. A key challenge for the soulful leader is being able to move from a "telling posture" to an "asking posture." That is, soulful leaders no longer hand out orders. Instead they help people discover and take next steps.

Creating a coaching culture begins with the leadership.

Soulful leaders are coaches who believe the best answers are within the collective voice of employees, clients, and members rather than from the edicts of a board or staff directive.

Soulful leaders are confident that the skills, insights, gifts, abilities, and experiences of those they are leading are valuable in making things better and improving the quality of relationships, products, or effort.

Soulful leaders who are building a coaching culture also acknowledge that the passion and callings of those they lead are critical parts of moving the organization and system forward. They trust that the right persons are in the organization for taking the next steps, steps that they can embrace, nurture, and live into. *Good to Great*, Jim Collins' powerful book about organizational change, suggests that at times the "wrong people are on the bus" and therefore prohibit or sabotage change. If this is discovered, Collins suggests getting the "wrong people off the bus and the right people on the bus."[1] Collins' approach may be necessary at times, but we suggest that those wanting to create change through a coach approach take a different approach to dissenters.

Emptiness represents the absence of something.

The Soulful Leader's Response to Dissenters/Skeptics

Soulful leaders understand what William Bridges calls a "neutral zone." Bridges says this "gap in the continuity of existence" comes about because "emptiness represents the absence of something."[2]

"So when the something is as important as relatedness and purpose and reality, we try to find ways of replacing these missing elements as quickly as possible," Bridges says. "The neutral zone is not an important part of the transitional process—it is only a temporary state of loss to be endured."[3]

We believe that this neutral zone creates time and space for rebirthing—for personal reflection, meditation, and making shifts that matter. It's the time when you pay attention to "that new baby kicking" that allows you the space and opportunity to embrace the new and the risks of the new. It's the time that we have to self-manage ego and demands of our fast-paced lives, allowing us to pull forth new disciplines and new realities.

As a soulful leader, you will find skeptics in the organization who oppose the idea of change, the threat of change, the process of change, or the expected results of change. For instance, note how President Obama deals with his dissenters—he surrounds himself with persons who disagree so they will challenge his thinking. A soulful leader will consider these questions about those who seem opposed to change:

The soulful leader listens to dissenters.

- What do they see that I do not see?
- What do they see that others do not see?
- What are the issues of most concern to them now? In the future?
- What can we learn from their concerns?
- What needs to happen for them to buy into the shifts?
- How can we create a win/win without sabotaging the mission?
- What's missing from the dialogue about change?
- How can those who are opposed to change or rocked by change move from pain to purpose to passion?
- What avenues can be created to relieve the pain and discomfort of change and open doors to renewed purpose and intense passion?

Move from pain to purpose to passion.

As a way of self-management, the soulful leader considers the questions carefully. This opens the leader up to the reality that those who are skeptics might be good teachers who can strengthen the needed shifts being called for so that transformation can occur. Far too often leaders consider those who oppose change as enemies and threats rather than teachers and potential strategists who can help make the change more meaningful and relevant to the organization.

After personally reflecting on the skeptics and what they might be able to bring to the dialogue, the soulful leader turns directly to those who might be touched by change—directly or indirectly. In so doing, the leader may reframe those same questions and ask them directly of those most affected. The learnings from this internal and external dialogue are certain to bring greater clarity on most if not all the issues and build some ownership of and practical solutions to the challenges and opportunities ahead.

Harmony emerges as opinions are shaped, voiced, and heard. Effective soulful leaders are called to be healthy and skilled coaches in times of stress and great diversity of opinion, demographics, or value systems and traditions. Let's explore who a coach is, then delve deeper into what a coach does.

Coaches Step into Healthy Soulful Leadership

Coaching demands great self-awareness and comfort with who you are as a leader. Coaches have a keen sensitivity and ability to read a group and move the group toward contextualized answers to their unique challenges.

Soulful leadership steps up to the challenge of coaching and learning curves brought by change. Ruth Haley Barton discusses the challenges leaders often face:

> Such moments come to all of us—moments when our leadership feels like something we "put on" like a piece of clothing pulled out of the closet for a particular occasion rather than something that flows from a deep inner well fed by a pure source. Perhaps you are preparing a presentation and you have the sinking realization that you are getting ready to exhort others in values and behaviors you are not living yourself. Maybe you are a leader and notice that more and more frequently you are manufacturing a display of emotion because it has been too long since you have experienced any real authenticity. Or perhaps someone needs care and you realize you just don't care. You rally your energy to go through the motions, but you know that your heart is devoid of real compassion.[4]

Soulful leaders walk into their discomfort and their fears to lead people and groups forward. Barton brings further clarification when she declares:

> The soulful leader pays attention to such inner realities and the questions that they raise rather than ignoring them and continuing the charade or judging himself or herself harshly and thus cutting off the possibility of deeper awareness. Spiritual leadership emerges from our willingness to stay involved with our own soul— that place where God's Spirit is at work stirring up

Harmony emerges as opinions are shaped, voiced, and heard.

Coaching demands great self-awareness and comfort with who you are as a leader.

our deepest questions and longings to draw us deeper into relationship. Staying involved with our soul is not narcissistic navel gazing; rather, this kind of attentiveness helps us stay on the path of becoming our true self—a self that is capable of an ever-deepening yes to God's call on our life.

Barton continues:

The settings in which many of us are trying to provide leadership are places where everyone is crashing through the woods together, harried and breathless, staying on the surface of the intellect and the ego while all things soulful flee deeper into the woods. Besides that, we know that the leader is often the one who gets shot or voted off the island. The savvy soul knows better than to run out into a clearing, thereby giving everyone a better shot![5]

Soulful leadership that functions creatively and spiritually in the midst of paradox is not for the faint of heart. It is much easier to give in to one polarity or the other. Peter Senge notes:

Emotional tension can always be relieved by adjusting the one pole of the creative tension that is completely under our control at all times—the vision. The feelings that we dislike go away because the creative tension that was their source is reduced. Our goals are now much closer to our reality. Escaping emotional tension is easy—the only price we pay is abandoning what we truly want, our vision.

A spiritual leader is not willing to merely escape the emotional tension; rather, he/she has the stamina and staying power to remain in that place of creative tension until a third way opens up that somehow honors both realities.[6]

Coaches need to be aware of these leadership characteristics in themselves and those they are coaching. A coach is called to self-manage personal agendas, opinions, and judgments. The person or group being coached dictates the agenda. The coach, however, listens and watches for patterns: what's working and what's not working, along with what is being avoided or ignored. The coach's job is to connect dots that move the person or group forward in their tasks.

Relationship is the first and most important principle in coaching. James Flaherty says, "Relationship is the background for all coaching efforts. The relationship must be one in which there is mutual respect, trust and mutual freedom of expression."[7]

Flaherty insists that the products of coaching include long-term excellent performance, self-correction, and self-generation.[8]

> A spiritual leader is not willing to merely escape the emotional tension.

Distinctives of Leading through Coaching

Let's unpack some of the distinctives of leading through coaching. How do you become an excellent coach and a soulful leader? Some needed skills can be seen in how leaders FACE change, MAKE change, and EMBRACE change. This awareness must occur in order to navigate through transitions to authentic transformation. Consider these options and the accompanying coaching questions.

Leaders Must FACE Change

Coaching to FACE change involves:

- Fear
- Acceptance
- Community
- Evaluation/Exploration

Leaders must **FACE** change

Fear
Acceptance
Community
Evaluation/
   Exploration

Fear

Fear is extremely powerful. Personal fear keeps you stuck. Fear can keep you in old patterns and habits that can sabotage the future, even pull you backward. Human nature wants to remain in comfortable old familiar places, even if these places might be dangerous for us. Fear is the opposite of love. To truly love ourselves and allow good things to happen proves more challenging than we think. Iyanla Vanzant, a true inspirer and life coach, states:

> People develop habits. They do certain things, in certain ways, not because that is the only way they can be done. Rather they act in certain ways because human beings are habitual. Let's face it, we are easily trained, habitual creatures who become comfortable doing certain things in a particular way. If we want to be honest, we would have to admit that the way we do the things we do is more often than not an attempt to avoid pain, discomfort, and unfamiliarity, not necessarily in pursuit of doing things the best way or the right way—if there is such a thing. Taking this into consideration, we can honestly say that as human beings, we don't always do the right thing. We cut corners. We tell little fibs. We do what we think we must do to save ourselves. We react to many life situations in fear, with a fear response. This is normal and true for most human beings.[9]

Pain is a pathway to growth.

Pushing through fear to activate faith and take next steps is where coaching can play a key role. Sensing fear in the environment, the attentive coach will ask questions to lead the way out of fear:

- What is keeping you stuck?
- What causes you to be afraid?
- What is the ultimate destination if you stay on the road you're on now?
- Why are you avoiding the inevitable?
- What would be the likely result if you could walk into your fear now?

Acceptance

The process of change and movement forward cannot be done alone.

Part of pressing on and pushing through the fear of change is *accepting reality*: things really are not working for you and/or your organization. Accepting this true reality and beginning to be totally honest will bring the true power for change and the innovative spirit. Often this acceptance and lifting of the denial wrapped around a situation cannot be done without a coach or another outside perspective. We have often heard of not being able to see the forest for the trees. All objectivity is often lost if we continue to stay isolated, disconnected from change, and away from honest feedback. The trained coach will ask:

What does change look like to you?

- What will it take to allow you to accept that change is needed?
- What does that change look like to you?
- What new skills, attitudes, and behavior are needed to start the change?
- What is the best version of yourself you can see now?

Community

The process of change and movement forward cannot be done alone. A healthy and balanced outside perspective is needed. A coach is going to enter a situation with an open mind, not with a preset, programmed plan of action. A good coach will have the attitude of "What will I learn from this new situation and coaching environment today?" In the coaching process the coach and the PBC (person being coached) are always learning. The coach will help the person or group see things more clearly and allow the group or person to think, reflect, and collaborate on new options and possibilities for moving into one's true purpose and positive change. The coach will present such questions as:

- Why do I avoid developing community and learning in community?
- What can I learn from others in this situation?
- What am I learning about myself in regard to my own attitude and beliefs?
- How does the feeling of healthy community and connection help when facing change?

Evaluation/Exploration

Pushing through the fear, accepting that change is needed and wanted, and beginning to articulate these findings with a coach *opens the path for exploration and evaluation.* One coach tells his clients, "You must give yourself permission to window shop." What a clever way to say, "Get out there! Try new things. Explore." This cycle of exploration and evaluation can be done in many different ways, depending on the group or individual. It may require small, focused, disciplined steps because too much change too quickly will turn the boat upside down. Or, a huge shift or leap of faith may be exactly what is needed to start one's new adventure. Could it be time to step out of one boat and get into a new one? A clever coach will offer the following questions:

- How do you begin to evaluate places to explore?
- What does your criteria include?
- What does exploration look like?

Soulful Leaders Must **MAKE** Change.

Movement
Adjustment
Kinesis
Evolution

Leaders Must MAKE Change

Coaching to MAKE change requires:

- Movement
- Adjustment
- Kinesis
- Evolution

Movement

One thing we definitely know as coaches is that *change requires movement and action.* A good friend is always encouraging, "Let's see a little less talk and a little more action." We look at each other and laugh. But, what a great reminder for all of us! Many of us cannot begin any movement until we F-A-C-E our reality and admit we are stuck or, in some cases, moving backward. We must ask:

- How do we know when we are stuck?
- Where does movement start?
- How do we know if we are moving in the right direction?

Adjustment

As movement begins, *many adjustments will be needed*. Personal adjustments and group dynamics begin to change. A coach will begin to walk you and/or the group through these transitions. They will prove much more difficult and powerful than you might think. These movements and adjustments will affect people differently. Some will experience great excitement and renewed interest and passion. Others will begin to "dig their feet in the sand" and say, "Hold on! I am not sure these changes need to happen." Some will become outright critics of change. The coach will lead the person or group to explore:

- What happens when adjustments begin to turn into conflict?
- When is conflict good?
- What can be learned through resolution of conflict?
- How will we incorporate those who strongly oppose change?

Kinesis

During the movement and adjustment phases, it is important to start paying close attention to what is pulling you and the group. What is feeding the passion and excitement for change? What is causing a drain or a tendency to pull back to the way things were? Are fear and uncertainty beginning to creep in and be saboteurs? When you are at this place, think about *what pulls you toward the Light (kinesis)*. Your true gifts and calling will fuel your passion and excitement, not drain it.

"Go to things and places that make your baby kick!"

One coach constantly says to his clients, "Go to things and places that make your baby kick!" Pregnant women often feel the kick of new life within them, bringing great hope, joy, and even—sometimes—fearful excitement and new energy for the rest of the journey. Embracing this energy and movement toward the things, people, and places that fuel your passion will sustain the momentum needed and make change a lot more fun. In the process of coaching you may need to deal with these questions:

- What makes your "baby kick"?
- What have you done today that makes you proud?
- What does moving into purpose and passion look like?
- Who can you stand beside and be your very best?
- Are we having fun yet?

Evolution

As the movement, adjustments, and kinetic process begin, you and/or your group will start the evolution of new ideas, beliefs, strategies, and goals. This is an exciting place to be. You will see old ideas and patterns begin to unravel and the integration of the old and the new begin to fuse together. This allows you to embrace your new world with much more courage and clarity. This progression is a big hope builder. You finally get to a place where you may not be certain where you are going, but you are sure that you do not want to go back to the way things were. This is a powerful tipping point for change. You are at the point of no return. There is no turning back. This is to be celebrated. As you do so, you will deal with these questions:

- How do you know your changes are turning into greater things and evolving?
- What pulls/tugs on you to return to your comfort zone?
- What fuels you to keep pressing on?
- What vision do you see down the road?

Leaders Must EMBRACE Change

Once leaders have started to F-A-C-E and M-A-K-E change, we then carry on, with the integration of old and new ideas, to embrace the new vision and world into which they are preparing to walk. John Trent calls this incremental transformation "two degree shifts." He explains, "It's the small marks on our soul that will shape our lives."[10]

Here are ways leaders EMBRACE change

- Experiment
- Manage/Maintain

Here are ways leaders **EMBRACE** change:

Experiment
Manage/Maintain
Build Bridges, not
   Barriers
Rebuild
Align
Challenge
Explode

- Build Bridges, not Barriers
- Rebuild
- Align
- Challenge
- Explode

Experiment

At this stage, you truly begin to experiment with your new skills, mind-set, and ideas. By now you have done some "window shopping," agreed on some things that you want to try, and agreed on some things that you do not want to try. You are not actually at the place where you know for certain what is going to work and what is not going to work, but enough exploration has been done that it is time to take some informed risks and next steps, and to experiment with some new ideas, programs, and events. As you do, ask:

With each "no" there is a death.

- What are you and/or your group willing to try?
- How do you know who tries what?
- How do you measure the success of your experiments?
- What changes have you declared off-limits? Why?

Explore ways to build bridges instead of barriers

Manage/Maintain

As these experiments begin to take place, a soulful coach will help the group determine who, what, when, and where. Just as in one's personal journey, an organization has to discern what it needs to let go of to move into a better purpose-filled life. You must quickly decide:

Looking for the win/win in a situation will increase your chances drastically for success.

- Who should manage what?
- What needs to be maintained? What needs to be birthed?
- What needs to go away or be terminated?
- Who must coordinate changes with whom? How?

Build Bridges, not Barriers

As you begin to make these decisions, you will discover that some will be extremely difficult. With each "no" there is a death. Many will struggle here and will not be willing to look at and weigh the costs. As you enter this phase, remember giving birth is often painful. Understand the need to explore ways to build bridges instead of barriers. A bridge is a connection between where you are and where you want to be—it can be a visual picture or an emotional reality that can be defined. A barrier, on the other hand, is something that prevents you from moving—it keeps you stuck in the current place—whether physical, spiritual, emotional, financial, or relational. Looking for the win/win in a situation will increase your chances drastically for success rather than constantly using your time and energy to work through obstacles and barriers. A coach will guide you to the answers to these questions:

- How would you define a barrier? a bridge?
- How do you build bridges instead of barriers?
- How do you define a win/win situation?
- Are you a bridge-builder or a barrier?

> Walking into the unknown and the unfamiliar takes us all out of our comfort zones.

Rebuild

As you experiment and manage bridges and barriers, it will be time to reflect and discuss how the rebuilding will look. You will definitely discover many things to rebuild as this process forces you to decide what to keep, what to change, and what to let go of as you move into your future. Coaching questions at this phase include:

> Alignment happens as awareness is deepened and heightened.

- How does one begin to rebuild? What pieces do you keep?
- What pieces do you let go of? What pieces do you keep, but remold?
- Do you need new pieces not available in your current organization?

Align

Walking into the unknown and the unfamiliar takes us all out of our comfort zones and thus the personal and group challenges continue. At this stage you will find the need to align your new choices (an intellectual decision) and discoveries with your intentional actions (an action based on your conscious decisions). You will then see your new world begin to take shape and unfold. This is living into your integrity. Alignment has to do with getting parts of life in sync that are out of sync. It might be a real disconnect or a perceived one. Alignment happens as awareness is deepened and heightened, options are explored, barriers and bridges are identified, and conscious decisions are made that move you from where you are to where you want to be. This will be exciting but will feel unfamiliar and uneasy at times (just think of the caterpillar turning into the butterfly). A coach will guide you in asking:

- What does realignment look like for you?
- How do you celebrate your successes as realignments begin?
- How do you learn from where you have "missed the mark"?
- What are your challenges at this point?

Challenge

Stockdale Paradox: You must maintain unwavering faith that you can and will prevail in the end.

Birthing the new carries challenge with it. Personal conflicts will surface, and decisions will need to be made. Anything worthwhile will require courage, discipline, and perseverance. As pioneers of change and change management, you will encounter many trials and tribulations.

Jim Collins states, "Every good-to-great company embraced what we came to call the Stockdale Paradox: You must maintain unwavering faith that you can and will prevail in the end, regardless of the difficulties, AND at the same time have the discipline to confront the most brutal facts of your current reality, whatever they might be."[11] The coach asks:

How do soulful leaders differ from other leaders? Internal shifts inside oneself are the starting point.

- Will you and/or your organization simply slip back into that old familiar comfort zone and not change?
- What elements in your organization are truly brutal facts?
- How will everyone handle this challenge? What is the cost of handling it? Of not handling it?
- Who will succeed, and who will fail? Why?

Explode

As coaches, we have seen this time and time again. As you F-A-C-E, M-A-K-E, and then E-M-B-R-A-C-E change and transition, a new world takes shape. Programs, events, organizations, and—more importantly—people explode into their potential, passions, and true calling. The "gold in the making" comes forth. People and organizations then go places and do things they could have never planned or imagined during the first steps of facing one's fears. In all these situations, internal shifts inside oneself are the starting point. In some situations, the internal shifts may first be caused by an external factor, but then true transformation begins through the embraced shifts from the inside out. *FaithCoaching: A Conversational Approach to Spiritual Formation* provides additional coaching tools and insights for those seeking transformation.[12]

- How do you keep walking into the new?
- How do you teach others what you have learned?
- Who has exploded with potential you did not recognize? How can they best serve the organization?
- Who has caught the passion of the new vision and can help others catch the passion?
- How do you stay strong/focused to keep/maintain growth and change?

Soulful leaders not only navigate the waters of change, but soulful leaders initiate the momentum for persons and organizations to explore their depths, their desires, and their hungers through powerful questions and personal reflections that enable them to FACE, MAKE, and finally EMBRACE change. Such an authentic journey yields fulfillment that brings transformation to their lives, and often to the families and organizations of which they are a part. There is a ripple effect. How do soulful leaders differ from other leaders? They lead from the heart and the head. They ask powerful questions, rather than tell or make personal declarations. Soulful leaders coach. They do not command. They lead by example. They walk the talk. Soulful leaders are more focused on transformation that lasts rather than just change for the moment.

Soulful leaders are more focused on transformation that will last than on change for the moment.

SECTION
TWO

The Implications of
Soulful Leadership

Soulful Leaders Put Heart into Managing Change

The first part of this book has introduced you to basic concepts used in professional coaching. These are only basic concepts. The more you practice them the more empowering and transformational they become for you and those you coach. The remainder of this book looks at the basic elements of coaching theory and practice.

In this chapter we will introduce you to a new lens through which to examine the pebbles of possible changes cast at us. The first part provides an introduction to coaching and its general principles and tools. The remainder of the chapter introduces a "Ripple model" and seven key questions that become elements in your toolkit that you can use to transform and make shifts without making destructive waves. The tools are transformational because they create and deepen the influence and impact of leaders, families, organizations, and churches. Leaders can use the new toolkit for working with the changes that you decide you or your organization need to encounter and to make shifts during the storms in your context. This coach approach allows you to enter the process from any angle you choose as you customize intentional responses to change.

Transformational tools create and deepen the influence and impact of leaders.

These times call for soulful leadership.

Making Shifts without Making Waves—Tools That Transform

The exponential changes of our time calls for more than leadership; these times call for soulful leadership. Leadership in days of crisis focuses on what works, what sustains, what is personal, and what encourages flexibility and accessibility, according to James Morrison.[1] The deep changes on our threshold call for leaders with deep souls—leaders with virtues of wisdom, integrity, discernment, hope, patience, perseverance, and intentionality. In these tough economic and challenging days soulful leaders more often than not are learning to lead in time of crisis and learning to use and maximize what is "in the box" rather than just focusing "outside" or "beyond the box." In this book, we are providing soulful leaders two valuable insights that will allow them to face the waves of change with clarity instead of compromise:

1. discernment and discovery rather than dread; and
2. faith and heart instead of fear.

The Coach Approach

Coaches work off of the words and situation of the client.

Coaching is a powerful tool. We quickly acknowledge that trying to write about coaching brings its challenges. *Coaching conversations* may be informal and brief. *Coaching relationships* are usually formal and involve a contract that is co-created with the person or group being coached.

We are limited to jump-starting coaching conversations or relationships with most of our writing because we do not have the other side of the conversation present. Coaches work off of the words and situation of the client. Coaches listen attentively, being fully present with the person or group being coached. So, know that much of what we introduce you to simply represents a way to jump start coaching conversations; nonetheless, the timely use of the concepts, tools, and skills we share brings powerful results and shifts. Try it and see what happens.

Determining coachability is critical.

Let's look at ways leaders can help their organizations through change. First, we will look at some basic coaching principles and guidelines that ensure you understand the nature of coaching. Then we will explain the Ripple model (as seen on page 40) that serves as a new framework, a new lens for coaching through change. The seven key questions and other models in the book and in the appendices form a coaching toolkit for the soulful leader.

This book is about using the coach approach to introduce and manage change through transitions to revolutionary transformation. The skills we will discuss are appropriate and functional in any system or life that is coachable.

What makes a person, group, or system coachable?

Determining Coachability

Perceptive leaders must determine the nature of change facing their organizations and the coachability factor that is or is not present. Determining coachability is critical. Using these skills in places that are not ready or healthy enough is likely to generate even more frustration. So what makes a person, group, or system coachable?

- Open to change
- Ready to move forward
- Healthy enough to act responsibly and learn
- Driven by dreams and not by fears
- Commitment to the journey
- Understanding and open to help from others
- Willing to explore, rather than avoid, needed shifts

Determining coachability

Five Coaching Skills

Coaching provides practical means to make that call. Effective leaders of twenty-first–century groups must become familiar with the five coaching skills shown in the acrostic **LEARN.**

- Listen. Leaders should focus on what people in their organization are saying, paying careful attention to not only what they say but the way it is said. Leaders also need to be aware of what employees feel and desire.
- Encourage. Those at the head of a group must offer support that leads to action. Making mistakes is OK. It is part of the process. A person who has made a mistake needs encouragement and assurance, not blame and guilt.
- Ask questions. Leaders who want to know what's happening must ask powerful questions and listen carefully to the answers without predisposition as to what is correct.
- Respond. Coaches are in the business of discovery and exploration and sometimes eliciting truth-telling. Leaders must respond with feedback that moves the organization forward.
- Negotiate action. Every coaching conversation ends with the person being coached having clarity on what he or she is supposed to do and when it is supposed to be accomplished. Groups, families, businesses, or churches that do not act will likely be swept away by the changing environment.[2]

LEARN
Listen
Encourage
Ask
Respond
Negotiate

Leaders can use the necessary skills described in the LEARN skill set to help their groups and individuals move forward and stay connected. This basic model is used in most every coaching conversation or coaching relationship. Those skills come together in various coaching models that can be found in coaching literature. Coaching models are taught in coach training programs such as Valwood Christian Leadership Coaching (www.valwoodcoaching. org) and Coach Approach Ministries (www.ca-ministries.com) and any organization that follows the ethics and standards of the International Coaching Federation (www.coachfederation. org). We would also refer you to www.kenblanchard.com, www. mcgheeproductivity.com, www.theonpurposecompany.com, www.internal-impact.com, or www.careercoachacademy.com.

Almost every coaching conversation or relationship includes these basic concepts. While utilizing these skills, the various models can be adjusted to various situations. One model coaches use is best remembered by the acrostic FAST.[3]

FAST
Focus
Action
Summarize
Track

- *Focus*. Coaches ask questions such as, "What's on your mind today?" and, "What do you want to accomplish during this conversation?" Leaders might ask questions such as, "What do we need to accomplish?" and, "What's the top issue facing us now?" Creating focus lets the group reach its goal without wasting time, energy, and previous learnings.
- *Action*. This determines what might be possible. Coaches ask questions such as, "What have you thought about doing?" and, "What might be your first step?" Leaders might ask, "What are our options?" and, "What do we need to do?"
- *Summarize*. Connecting the dots of the conversation helps the person being coached explore how the situation got to where it is. Coaches ask questions such as, "How'd we get here?" Leaders can ask, "What caused the current situation?" Another coaching question may be, "How will you recap or bottom line your take-aways?"
- *Tracking*. This helps the person being coached see the big picture. Coaches ask questions such as, "How does this play into your overall agenda?" Leaders might ask, "How does this fit into our mission?" Tracking is also used to bring in accountability. What is the client willing to do by the next coaching session?

While basic skills are presented here, we will build upon these in the pages to come as we apply these concepts to making shifts without making waves. What then are the benefits of using the coach approach to introducing and managing change as opposed to a leader imposing or declaring change on an organization?

Benefits of Coaching

Coaching can help others reinvent themselves to weather the storms of change. Leaders who coach can help their organizations

- Experience community, not cliques
- Explore truth together and unlock passion
- Move from indoctrination to inquiry
- Build community through storytelling, personal expression, and faith formation
- Create a multi-sensory experience that becomes a sacred place and space for persons to explore deep questions

- Foster stewardship that nurtures life, personal mission, and fulfillment of God's mission in the world
- Understand and embrace why change is needed
- Encourage people to tell their stories and connect with the stories of others
- Draw out experiences of the heart rather than exercises of the head
- Learn to weave relational, restorative, and redemptive threads that become the fabric out of which authentic experiences emerge

Advantages of Coaching

Coaching can have many advantages for organizations. Some can be best explained in the acrostic COACHING.

- *Connections*. Groups often function better when the members bond with each other. They do much greater things together than they could do separately. A leader serving as a coach helps the organization "connect the dots" of its problems, issues, and goals for movement forward together.
- *Options*. A coaching relationship enables an organization to look at options more quickly. In many cases, organizations are stuck. Remaining in the same cycle produces no change. Frustration and hopelessness can build and take over. Coaches prod the organization to discover its options to get out of the rut.
- *Action*. The coach approach encourages groups to "bottom line" their learnings and move them into action. In many cases people know what they should or should not be doing, but remain in a "no movement" zone. A coach adds the layer of accountability to the action.
- *Community*. In a group environment the coach can serve as the connector and bridge builder to the entire team. Many who have been coached say they would have never moved as quickly or embraced change as effectively without being coached.
- *Help*. Coaching includes a surrender piece. Members of the group must get their egos out of the way, allowing themselves to be coached. Everyone needs help in areas of life. Clients and organizations must grant permission and show willingness to be stretched and step outside their comfort zones.
- *Integration*. A leader using the coach approach assists the group in the integration of their decisions. The leader-coach helps the group explore the pros and cons of changes and decisions. Life-changing transitions cause

Benefits of Coaching

- Coaching can help others reinvent themselves.
- Coaching includes a surrender piece.
- Coaching is about helping the group find its true potential.

waves, and the shifts will need to be understood and embraced.

- *Negotiation*. The coaching environment enables members of the organization to realize where they have room to move and new areas to explore. Coaching will also enable them to list non-negotiables—places and things they are not willing to give up or change. A coach may or may not challenge some of the answers.
- *Gifts*. Coaching is about helping the group find its true potential, its calling and passions. Coaching is about helping the organization find healthy solutions and resources to move forward. Coaching helps plant seeds needed to build and grow with integrity and authenticity. Finding these gifts will enable everyone to feel truly alive and passionate for their contribution, efforts, and time. Jim Collins discusses "the Hedgehog concept": "This concept is not a goal to be the best, a strategy to be the best, an intention to be the best, or a plan to be the best. It is an understanding of what you can be the best at. The distinction is absolutely crucial."[4]

It is an understanding of what you can be the best at.

It is time to look closely at your own situation. Are you ready for the shifts of change that can guide your group or organization through the inevitable storms on the horizon? To do so you must be ready to lead your organization in answering the intense, powerful questions a coach will ask.

Consider these possible coaching questions.

- How would you describe our group?
- What's working?
- What would make the current situation better?
- What are we struggling with?
- What energizes us?
- What drains our energy?
- What would make things better?

Are you ready to listen to, accept, and act on the diverse answers to these questions that your group will produce? A coach will help you understand what is happening as your group delves into finding the shape of your company as it faces the storms and the shape it can shift to so as to maneuver safely around these storms.

The chart on page 37 is an adaptation of material often used in churches and nonprofit organizations. The coach can use the chart when the group is struggling to determine core values or to explore if what is being said actually lines up with what is being done.

What Is the Focus of Your Organization?

ATTRACTIONAL ORGANIZATION	MISSIONAL ORGANIZATION
Grow the organization	Impact the world/community
Time/tasks/Defined by (mission/objectives)	Restore/redeem broken people
Who is 'in/out' of the organization	Web of relationships inside and outside organization
Fish to keep (rod and reel) membership for retention	Fish & release (net) membership for mission activation
Come structures that focus only on institutional preservations	Go structures that focus beyond the institution to the mission of the organization
Building buildings and more organizational structures	Building relationships and people inside and outside the organization
Bounded (fence-like characteristics)	Centered (like a well found in midst of desert)
Homogeneous	Diversity

What is the focus of your organization?

The above chart[5] serves as a guide for self-assessment of an individual, group, or organization. Keeping in mind that balance is esssential, assess the percentage of each category that fits your group. A coach might simply provide the chart and ask:

1. What category best describes your group organization?
2. How would you evaluate your organization?
3. How does your daily activity attune with your previous answers?
4. How do your daily activities honor your mission statement?
5. What would help you to be more attuned as an organization now?
6. Who can help you make the needed shifts?
7. What are the shifts you believe need to be made to improve your effectiveness over the next six months?

Rather than creating waves when shifts are presented, how can leaders influence, open new doors, and rethink and refocus beliefs and priorities? A soulful leader relies heavily upon the

LEARN (Listen, Encourage, Ask, Respond, Negotiate) skills and basic coaching models such as FAST (Focus, Action, Summarize, Tracking) to coach persons forward who might be stuck and in a defensive posture.

A New Lens—The Ripple Model

The Ripple model is all about creating flexibility and personalization while sustaining momentum during times of change and challenge. The Ripple model is based on the image of a pebble being thrown in a pond, creating waves of hope, direction, encouragement, and inspiration for moving forward. We suggest six entry points (where the conversation starts) for using this model. Understand that these entry points will likely not be sequential. An entry point is simply where a person or organization chooses to enter a coaching conversation. It may be with a pinch or challenge they are experiencing; or, an entry point could be a project or task that needs to be completed but is currently not happening. The coach often learns much just by where the person or group chooses to begin the coaching conversation. The entry point often reveals values, rituals, traditions, blind spots, or deficits that are to be addressed or clarified.

> 1. Openness to change
> 2. Learning to face the unfamiliar
> 3. Self-awareness/clarity
> 4. Creating forward movement that creates momentum
> 5. Commitment to forward movement and community
> 6. Moving beyond denial to face reality

These elements of the Ripple model are simply suggestive of some of the probable ripples created by the pebbles of change being cast in the tranquility of one's life or organization. This model is primarily a framework for the coach to listen to the person being coached for entry points, disconnects, and what's missing. Using this model, the coach listens for internal or external shifts the person is facing. As these shifts are discussed, explained, and clarified, the coach or leader can determine their focus, which is the first part of the FAST model.

The new lens of the Ripple model provides a new way of active listening, learning and assessing the situation. These new methods are part of the soulful leader's new toolkit.

Other parts of the toolkit are resources, strategies, powerful questions for building ownership, understanding, support, and an expanded leadership base focused on moving the person or group forward in effectiveness and relevancy. The new toolkit helps new dreams come alive to move through change in a way that moves individuals from pain to purpose, from wandering to walking, and organizations from maintenance to mission to capacity building.

The ripple model is all about creating flexibility and personalization while sustaining momentum.

An entry point is where the conversation begins.

The entry point often reveals values, rituals, traditions, blind spots or deficits.

The models and powerful coaching questions are designed to tap into the heart of the leader and the others in the organization in ways that transform not only the persons, but also the families and organizations in which they are involved.

Tools for Aligning Life and Purpose

The soulful leader's new toolkit includes avenues for aligning life and purpose in ways that deepen the influence and the impact that fuels the transformation:

- *Seven powerful key coaching questions* empower persons or organizations faced with change.
- Resources unpack the implications and strategies for the person or group being coached.
- Applications are created for the context based on the personal or organizational mission statement or purpose.
- The *value of the Ripple model* is that it provides a filter through which to listen and a lens through which to look at the real situation before you.
- The seven key powerful questions provide ways to get others onboard, clarify their understanding, enlist new leaders, and explore possible blind spots and organizational implications.
- We also provide in the soulful leaders toolkit other coaching models. These will help the coach or the client retain focus. The models allow them to gain traction after getting stuck when faced with *BARRIERS* or find a need to build some *BRIDGES*.

The new toolkit helps new dreams come alive.

Coaching is not necessarily a linear process with predetermined questions leading to a planned conclusion. The best coaching is flexible and follows the issues of the person being coached. If a coach listens carefully, the person will reveal the next question he or she needs to be asked.

The coach listens for internal or external shifts the person is facing.

The seven key questions, the *Ripple* model, and the *BARRIERS* and *BRIDGES models* to which we will introduce you in the next chapters can be used in any order that best serves the person or group being coached. The reality that coaching is a non-linear leadership process is often the biggest challenge for most groups and leaders, but it may be one challenge worth facing as different generations, with differing learning styles, enter leadership. It is more an art than science. However, if you are working with a linear thinker or group, these models can be shared with them to help them follow and engage the coaching process. Remember, great coaching follows the energy and learning style of the person being coached. You can do it—practice and use the *Making Shifts without Making Waves* learning cards found in the appendices. Also study the coaching guide available at www.soulful-leadership.com.

Now let's look at the Ripple model. We will use this model in the remainder of the book.

Ripple Model for Coaching Individuals and Organizations

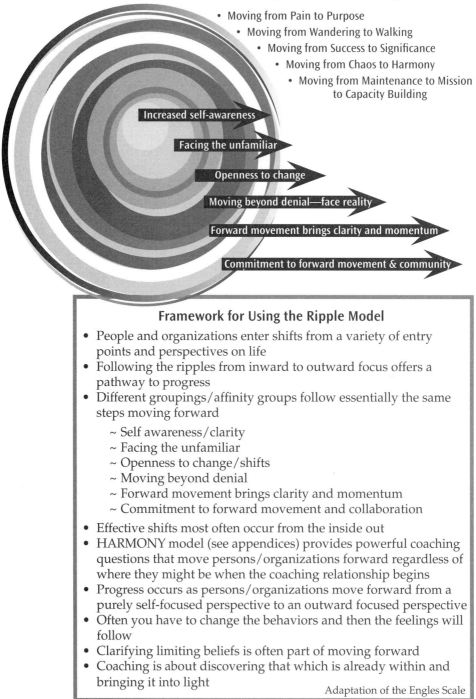

- Moving from Pain to Purpose
- Moving from Wandering to Walking
- Moving from Success to Significance
- Moving from Chaos to Harmony
- Moving from Maintenance to Mission to Capacity Building

Increased self-awareness

Facing the unfamiliar

Openness to change

Moving beyond denial—face reality

Forward movement brings clarity and momentum

Commitment to forward movement & community

Framework for Using the Ripple Model

- People and organizations enter shifts from a variety of entry points and perspectives on life
- Following the ripples from inward to outward focus offers a pathway to progress
- Different groupings/affinity groups follow essentially the same steps moving forward

  ~ Self awareness/clarity
  ~ Facing the unfamiliar
  ~ Openness to change/shifts
  ~ Moving beyond denial
  ~ Forward movement brings clarity and momentum
  ~ Commitment to forward movement and collaboration

- Effective shifts most often occur from the inside out
- HARMONY model (see appendices) provides powerful coaching questions that move persons/organizations forward regardless of where they might be when the coaching relationship begins
- Progress occurs as persons/organizations move forward from a purely self-focused perspective to an outward focused perspective
- Often you have to change the behaviors and then the feelings will follow
- Clarifying limiting beliefs is often part of moving forward
- Coaching is about discovering that which is already within and bringing it into light

Adaptation of the Engles Scale

Diversity of demographics, families, rituals, and traditions—along with decreasing funding through traditional venues, and accompanied by an increasingly secular culture—is creating storms for many churches, judicatories, and denominations these days.

A declining local congregation in a metropolitan area called for help with these issues that were creating great internal stress for staff and congregation—most of whom wanted to go back "to the good ole' days" when their style of worship, music, and programming drew the people into membership. Now the external changes are such that their familiar traditions, music, and worship styles are no longer attracting or even retaining their membership. Their historic congregation is losing face in the community and among their denomination because they are no longer seen as effective.

The new lens of the Ripple model provides a new way of active listening, learning, and assessing the situation.

The coach approach has been more than helpful in diffusing the power struggles in this church, while inviting the members to clarify their mission, values, and next steps. It is amazing to use the coach approach and watch the power struggles dissolve, ownership grow as questions are addressed by the group, and new options and possibilities come into view. (Refer to the framework of ripple model).

Moving beyond Denial/Facing New Reality

This congregation finds it almost overwhelming to embrace their new realities of demographics, funding, leadership, and growing disconnects with their culture. However, the coach approach, along with some consulting, allows them to "stop fighting/debating" long enough to "explore and dream together." The energy the coach approach created in the room brought "hope and the beginning of some healing," according to some of their key leaders.

Openness to Change/Shifts

Once some clarity broke through and new realities were beginning to be embraced, some opened themselves to change and at least a willingness to explore what shifts in worship, leadership, music, and programming this might involve. It was not a commitment to do it, but at least willingness to explore feasible options.

Facing the Unfamiliar

As time and coaching proceeded with key leaders, and as questions and push backs were addressed by the group, two key leaders declared, "I'm willing to try this—even though it's very different—if it will help our church!" This was a breakthrough that generated energy among the group. We then worked to focus on what was realistic and what were they willing to experiment with now.

Self-Awareness/Clarity

The new clarity and increased self-awareness that emerged was frightening to many, and built hope for others. It was increasingly evident in the group of key leaders that labeling their challenges, rather than just feeling them, proved strengthening for them and supplied enough energy and hope to grapple with possibilities.

Forward Movement Brings Clarity and Momentum

Labeling some fears and embracing some possibilities gave way to experiments that built hope and momentum for the group. You could feel the ownership of building the "new." Even while flying the plane, they were willing to rebuild it. You could see the joy and sense of team emerging. They were having fun!

Commitment to Forward Movement Builds Community and Collaboration

It's amazing to see the impact of a few good successes. They were not only having fun creating the new, but they were also experiencing the realities that the new was working! Their new dreams could become realities! The great "Aha" has been that they can continue to have their traditional programming and needs met, too, as they learn the values and skills of creating parallel structures around similar core values. They also learn to embrace that, over time, this allows their founding core values to be expressed differently to the new generation. In this way, when the existing church culture dies out (and it is dying out rapidly), a new church with similar core values will continue to exist in that community. Wow! How amazing!

Passing through Business/Nonprofit Storms

Over a decade ago Jim Collins, in his best-selling book, introduced us to companies that moved from *Good to Great*. Many of those powerful companies have moved from *Good to Great* to Gone… Many have dissolved, filed for bankruptcy, or reinvented themselves to move beyond the economic challenges, lack of accountability, and deficiencies in integrity that contributed to their downfall.[6] Companies, all over the world, are being threatened by a number of external and internal realities that are putting companies at high risk.

It is our hope and belief that the principles of the coach approach to soulful leadership can restore strength amidst weakness and restore integrity, accountability, and increased revenue amidst confusion and distrust. As companies and corporations

Dimensions of the Ripple Model:

- Moving beyond Denial/Facing New Reality
- Openness to Change/Shifts
- Facing the Unfamiliar
- Self-Awareness/ Clarity
- Forward Movement Brings Clarity and Momentum
- Commitment to Forward Movement Builds Community and Collaboration

begin their rebuilding of integrity, financial and client bases leaders will move into and beyond the basic principles of change and transition to transformation of leaders, who in turn can transform the business world.

Possible Shifts and How to Make Them Happen

Transition is about the soft skills and feeling issues. Change is about moving the structure, core values, and leadership forward to more effective service for a rapidly changing world. Creating change is a balancing act with built-in risks, but it is possible if you work the questions and build the ownership.[7] People do not mind change nearly as much if they just understand why change is proposed. The process works even better when the people are allowed to design the changes they feel are needed at that time. Spiritual discernment is a key part of finding the right time and people, so pray and listen and observe "all things."

> People do not mind change nearly as much if they just understand why change is proposed.

Seven Key Coaching Questions

The Seven Key Coaching Questions are available for those who want to make shifts without making waves. These are framed in the form of powerful coaching questions because leaders who ask questions give the group being coached the power of the agenda. Here then are the "Seven Keys" for *Making Shifts without Making Waves* that lead to heartfelt change.

1. What are the shifts needed? (and which are needed right now?)
2. What are the shifts about anyway?
3. Who needs to know about the shifts?
4. What about the dissenters/skeptics?
5. What timing is needed?
6. Who can help us move forward now?
7. What is next?

Powerful Coaching Questions Build Clarity, Focus, and Ownership

As awareness grows and decisions are made, the next steps are discovered and often owned. Building ownership and clarity and creating a landmark (a marker that signals progress) are critical. This takes time, patience, and skill—along with determination, reflection, and focus. The toolkit is found to be useful in the timeliness of working through each of the key questions with key leaders, families, and decision makers. This must be done in a methodical, intentional, and mindful manner, being sensitive to feelings while being clear about needed change.

> The models and powerful coaching questions are designed to tap into the heart of the leader and clients.

Consider the powerful key coaching questions as tools for finding clarity and focus, as you build ownership and understanding among all key decision makers. We introduce you to the seven powerful questions here and will apply them in the remaining chapters.

Key 1: What are the shifts needed?

This question opens up great conversations that immediately reveal what people value and what is working for them and what is not working for them or those they love. Discovering together what shifts are needed for an organization to be more effective is key. Finding unanimity on this issue is most probably impossible.

Key 2: What are the shifts about anyway?

Once the needed shifts are listed by key persons, you might then prioritize them by inviting the group to vote on the top five that would make the most difference and most impact in reaching persons or organizational goals they currently find unreached. After the five are identified, list all the reasons these shifts are needed. Invite the group into this dialogue, and write these reasons for all to see on newsprint. This opens the door then for what others need to know to value the shifts as much as those in the dialogue.

Key 3: Who needs to know about the shifts?

Hopefully, you already have most of the key leaders, decision makers, and key family members involved in the dialogue. Ask that group: Who else needs to know about this? Invite those who mention the names of others to approach them prayerfully and intentionally to raise their awareness of these issues and to get their feedback. Often those in the initial dialogue become legitimizers for others in the organization. Use that relationship wisely but intentionally.

Key 4: What about the dissenters/skeptics?

It is very unlikely that everyone in a group or in a church will agree with all the proposed changes. Do not let this stop you. Many churches and organizations that are dying let the fragile feelings of a few stop the forward progress for many. Give the dissenters an opportunity to voice their concerns. Ask them what they need to know to buy in. Let them know that you will be sure their opinions are shared with the entire decision-making groups. This is tough but essential.

Key 5: What timing is needed?

Timing is everything in change and transition. Change, in most cases, does not need to happen overnight. If the utilities and mortgages cannot be paid due to lack of participation, it may require radical change. Otherwise patience, prayer, and intentionality are needed. Craft a realistic time line for making change happen. Invite others to respond to this with their insights and concerns. They often have ideas many have missed.

Key 5
What timing is needed in making these shifts?

Key 6: Who can help move us forward?

Change and transition will not happen if it all depends on just one leader or decision-making board. As more people buy into and have ownership of the new dream, a more effective and efficient new wave will emerge. Who are those you have discovered in the previous gatherings that have passion for the new? How can they help make this dream a reality? This system sounds simple in some ways, but it works. Bathe it in prayer, reflection, and intentionality. It really is possible to make shifts without making overwhelming waves. Follow the keys, use more questions than declarations, and build ownership based on the heart and the relationships persons have with those who are disappointed or disenfranchised from the organization.

Key 6
Who can help us move forward now?

Key 7: What is next?

The coach approach is a forward-looking process that seeks to move organizations and leaders forward. In a way, it is a never-ending process. Soulful leaders help their organizations think about the immediate future as they consider the next step.

Key 7
What is next?

With these questions in mind, let's look at how the coach approach provides the framework through which individuals and organizations can grow and thrive.

Soulful Leadership

Making Shifts That Matter in Individuals

Our previous book focused primarily on the church. *Reaching People Under 40 While Keeping People Over 60: Being Church for All Generations* (Chalice Press, 2007) has been very well received. It surfaces many leadership issues and challenges for church leaders. *Making Shifts without Making Waves* seeks to provide leaders of all types of organizations and from all walks of life additional understanding of the coach approach to introducing and managing change that yields transformation. In effect, our previous book exemplified the value of the coach approach to a specific issue. This book explains how the coach approach can be used to deal with a wide range of issues regarding introducing and managing change and transition for the purpose of transformation.

> When it comes to transformation, introducing and managing change is critical.

Revolutionary Transformation Evolves from Mindful and Heartfelt Shifts

Revolutionary Transformation = Change + Transition

When it comes to the business of transformation, introducing and managing change is critical. Many leaders are inexperienced, uninformed, and/or unable to introduce effective change, much less create space for transformation. Many pastors and leaders do not have the gifts or the calling to be leaders. They usually come to a church under job descriptions particularly crafted by church leaders to be sure the pastor will care for them, teach them, shepherd them, and manage programs for them. Rarely does a pastoral ministry description focus on leadership and introducing and managing change. That is usually the farthest thing from the minds of those on the minister search committee, but often it is the skill set the church needs most to move forward.

The best leaders for initiating and managing change are soulful leaders who follow their hearts rather than just their heads. We discussed the distinctives of the soulful leader earlier in the book.

Now that we have looked at the distinctives of a soulful leader and coach, it's time to explore some models you can use as a soulful leader to coach individuals through change and transition while maintaining as much attunement as possible. Finding the harmony in many situations can be challenging and awkward at best, especially where there is resistance to, disconnection from, and misunderstanding of the change taking place. To capture the harmonious nature of any situation, one first must be able to see and embrace the cause and effect of the decisions and progression for the shifts taking place. In these discoveries, the coach is looking for "the coachable moments." Harmony can be captured in the dialogue during these moments. Jane Creswell, master certified coach and author of *The Complete Idiot's Guide to Coaching for Excellence,* defines the coachable moment as when a person is in a position to benefit from learning something new related to a specific focus area and is ready to take action on it.[1] People and organizations need to know why change is happening. Finding the authentic coachable moments is a big part of this process.

Change and transition are two chief ingredients of most shifts that occur in people, teams, and organizations. In this chapter we want to explore with you the coach approach to making shifts that matter in individuals. These are critical ingredients of transformation.

Dictionary.com helps us differentiate between change and transition.

Change is defined at Dictionary.com in several ways. Among them are:

1. to make the form, nature, content, future course, etc., of [something] different from what it is or from what it would be if left alone.
2. to transform or convert to.
3. to substitute another or others for; exchange for something else, usually of the same kind.

According to the Web site, **transition** is "movement, passage, or change from one position, state, stage, subject, concept, etc., to another; change."

In other words, change has to do with the hard side—the structure, organization, furniture, etc. **Transition** is more the soft

---

The best leaders for initiating and managing change are soulful leaders who follow their hearts rather than just their heads.

Finding the authentic coachable moments is a big part of this process.

Change and transition are two chief ingredients of most shifts.

side, the human element—the feelings, attitude, and emotions of change. Transformation is a matter of the heart and head integration that impacts change and transition. William Bridges states, "You find yourself coming back in new ways to old activities, when you're in mindful transition."[2] He further declares, "The process of **transformation** is essentially a death and rebirth process rather than one of mechanical modification."[3]

Change and transition are the keys for external and internal shifts that need to occur for soulful transformation in individuals and groups. This is usually not an easy and clearly defined process from the beginning. It is normally a bit chaotic. This process is much more organic and evolves and unfolds as people make discoveries and have their "aha" moments of deeper understanding and clarity.

Bridges states, "Chaos is not a mess, but rather it is the primal state of pure energy to which the person returns for every true beginning."[4] *It is important for us to reframe our beliefs and thoughts around chaos to see that it serves as a starting point for the opportunity of real transformation.* Creation starts with chaos and a real sense of dis-ease! Chaos then moves to nothing (neutral zone) then to new creation.

You will have to endure times of uncertainty and doubt. Times of movement forward and times for reflection and sitting still will be required. This neutral zone, or what Iyanla Vanzant calls "in the meantime" is extremely important for saying goodbye to the old and having fertile soil for the new to begin. Bridges says another "reason for the gap between the old life and the new life is that the process of disintegration and reintegration is the source of renewal."[5] One might even say, "the message is in the mess."

Shifts Involve "in the Meantime" and Neutral Zone Strategies

Vanzant writes:

There are hundreds of thousands of meantime scenarios that give depth and meaning to life. The meantime between jobs, the meantime between the argument and the reconciliation, between the separation and the divorce, between the test and the results. Each of these meantime experiences, although fraught with anxiety and stress that make them seem unbearable, are emotionally and spiritually profitable. A honeymoon is a meaningful meantime. Likewise, the period of labor preceding a birth is a meaningful but painful meantime. There are those meantimes which are immediately identifiable as being worthwhile and empowering, and there are those that wreak havoc on the soul. In the meantime, the clock stops and you are put on God's divine schedule.[6]

Transformation is a matter of the heart and head integration that impacts change and transition.

You find yourself coming back in new ways to old activities when you're in mindful transition.

Move through fears to fulfillment.

The process of transformation is essentially a death and rebirth process rather than one of mechanical modification.

Creation starts with chaos and a real sense of dis-ease!

Clearly, the human side, the emotional side of change, is often the most difficult and challenging. Change is more often than not an emotionally charged issue. People have emotional connections to places, times, events, traditions, rituals, and "the way we have always done it." Being sensitive to this and helping persons to make these connections often dissolves emotional reactions, or at least helps them find the root of the emotional reaction to change.

The following concentric model is a visual representation of the ripples that are often created through a coach approach that moves the individual or organization forward from a closed posture with an inward/self-centered focus to a focus that has more of a systemic outward/missional focus. In today's world we are moving from a missional focus (outward focus) to an incarnational focus (integrating head and heart focus) where persons must experience the new to fully embrace the new (the change or transitions encountered). As coaches, we work with many individuals who find themselves needing to move from pain to purpose, wandering to walking, and from success to significance. Creating waves of hope and direction is the purpose of a soulful leader and the essence of coaching through the Ripple model. Explore how it might be used to create shifts in you.

> Times of movement forward and times for reflection and sitting still will be required.

> Change is more often than not an emotionally charged issue.

Ripple Model for Coaching Individuals

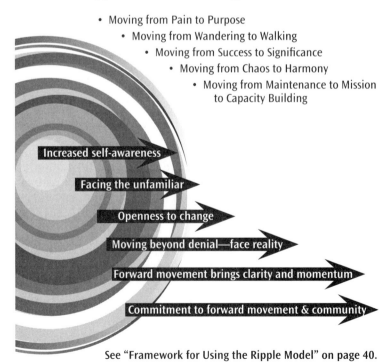

- Moving from Pain to Purpose
  - Moving from Wandering to Walking
    - Moving from Success to Significance
      - Moving from Chaos to Harmony
        - Moving from Maintenance to Mission to Capacity Building

Increased self-awareness

Facing the unfamiliar

Openness to change

Moving beyond denial—face reality

Forward movement brings clarity and momentum

Commitment to forward movement & community

See "Framework for Using the Ripple Model" on page 40.

Seven Keys for Making Shifts without Making Waves

1. What are the shifts needed? (and which are needed right now?)
2. What are the shifts about anyway?
3. Who needs to know about the shifts?
4. What about the dissenters/skeptics?
5. What timing is needed?
6. Who can help us move forward now?
7. What is next?

When coaching individuals around the storm of moving from pain to purpose, wandering to walking, or from success to significance, *it is important to realize that some external shifts often occur only after internal shifts have been made.* Sometimes these internal shifts start on their own or begin with a bit of nudging from others or from life experiences. However, in many situations, external factors and simply "life's hand" occur that demand our attention (without asking) and force us to focus on change. These "kairos moments" (divine appointments in the fertile soil of life lessons) test our character, integrity, soulfulness, and willingness to embrace this transformational moment. Change without transformation is simply an act of "moving the furniture" around. The more we change the more we stay the same.

> It is important to realize that some external shifts often occur only after internal shifts have been made.

> Kairos moments (divine appointments in the fertile soil of life lessons) test our character, integrity, soulfulness, and willingness to embrace this transformational moment.

Examples of the Impact of the Coach Approach on Individuals

An internal shift can be seen in a computer company executive who is extremely successful with his career and running his business unit, but longs for more. His self-awareness seems to be high, and he seems open. So he can be coached around options and forward movement. His financial success, corporate title, and responsibilities were simply no longer fulfilling. He is ready to *move from success to significance.* His passion and calling is to help lessen illiteracy around the world by getting books to those in need. You might even discover that a coaching conversation might include the themes from the show on NBC *The Philanthropist.* Sometimes clients, if they are visual learners, can take an objective story line of a television show and find alignments or challenges that they are willing to explore.

Another coaching client was filled with pain and lacking a clear purpose. How does this person get untangled from the bondage of addictive and dysfunctional behaviors that continue to rob him of freedom, healthy relationships, and fulfillment of his destiny? After coaching, he now declares, "I have had a long, painful journey that has helped me understand the human condition and our nature to sabotage. I continue to this day to push forward, live by lessons learned, and embrace the power of living authentically and being a person of integrity."

This client further explains, "If you took a look at my professional resume, one may say that I have had a good life and some success. I held positions with companies that paid well; management positions and some positions where I have been an individual contributor. I have had jobs that I loved and jobs that I have truly hated. Many told me, 'You have a job. You have a salary. Be happy.' For a person looking for more and going deeper in life's journey, this simply was not enough. My professional life was truly OK; however, my personal life was a mess! I was sick of the pain and eager to find my passion. For years, I was the perfect pretender, always wanting to please and not being honest with myself or others—doing things that I really did not want to do. Layers of anger and resentment were not being dealt with in a healthy way. I had relationships that were extremely toxic and experimented with many different kinds of drugs. My use of marijuana numbed my pain and anxiety while keeping me stuck in bad social circles and poor decision-making." In a case such as this, for a visual learner who might enjoy television a coach might explore a television show like *The Cleaner* (www.aetv.com/the-cleaner) on A&E television that provides an objective point of entry for some difficult coaching conversations. This show was inspired by the true story of real-life "extreme interventionist" Warren Boyd. The character modeled after him, named William Banks, is a recovering addict who is helping other addicts in their recovery. He struggles with his own commitment to his work and his love for family through an unusual relationship with God.

The client continues to explain the power of the coach approach in helping him untangle life and move from stuck to unstuck. "I had to *face the reality* that my life was not working the way I wanted it to work. I needed to change in order for things to change around me. That was a good first step, but change is difficult and I was not able to do it alone because I kept falling back into my old patterns. Ego and arrogance were barriers for me. It was two steps forward and one step back. Slowly and gradually, I terminated unhealthy friendships, stopped doing all drugs, and faced some solid walls around my *denial* and behaviors. It was becoming clear to me that my own decisions were keeping me from moving forward. As I slowly made changes and *faced the unfamiliar*, life began to open up. Everything was new! My old ways of coping did not work and I had lots to unlearn and then relearn a better and different way. Being a student of life, my lessons continue to deepen [and] bring *greater clarity* and understanding to the things that are truly important. I serve as a strong foundation to my family and friends now, I enjoy my

Change without transformation is simply an act of "moving the furniture around."

The more we change the more we stay the same.

coaching and training profession and being in service to others, and continue to be amazed at the exciting projects and *collaboration* that have opened to me as I continue to be better to myself and others. Things have opened up and all has happened through *community* and dialogue around my *openness* and willingness to confront my demons head on—teaching me surrender, gratitude, and the power of grace. As I continue to make good decisions, the doors of opportunity, fellowship, and collaboration keep growing. I have learned (the hard way) that staying open and honest and embracing my learnings one ripple at a time have carved out powerful learnings and shifts in me that, with the power of choice (making the right choices), will keep me moving in the right direction and living into my destiny." A portion of the client's journal clarifies the transformation that has emerged as he decided to deal with various "old ways of doing life" and the "new ways" that were emerging and giving him a fulfilling and balanced life he had never known.

Life-changing Shifts from Old Man to New Man, Using the Ripple Model

OLD	NEW
Stuck	Unstuck
Surviving	Living
Head *or* Heart	Head *and* Heart
Either/Or	Both/And
Floundering	Passion
Pain	Purpose
Addicted	Clean/Sober, but still an addict
Self-focused	Servitude
Avoiding	Confrontation

Dimensions of the Ripple Model:

- Moving beyond Denial/Facing New Reality
- Openness to Change/Shifts
- Facing the Unfamiliar
- Self-Awareness/Clarity
- Forward Movement Brings Clarity and Momentum
- Commitment to Forward Movement Builds Community and Collaboration

The shifts listed above represent many of the points of entry of coaching conversations. The lists also represents the power of coaching in moving people from where they are to where they want to be—without telling, but holding carefully their agendas in a sacred trust that empowers and encourages growth.

Moving from pain to purpose could be around leaving a painful relationship, leaving a job that one hates, a longing to spend more time with family, etc. Painful pinches can serve as the seedbed for tremendous growth and change. In all of these scenarios one must say good-bye to certain people, places, and things to have opportunity to say hello and welcome the new! One may reflect on the following questions as a self-assessment:

How did I get here?

What will energize me?

What brings me joy?

Who is this affecting?

Am I avoiding the inevitable?

Do I love myself and others enough to face my fears and change?

Here's another example. An external shift occurs with a smart, creative man who has had multiple successful jobs but was laid off from his last job. He is uncertain of what he wants to do next. He is very capable of doing many different things. He may or may not have good self-awareness, and he may be in denial over job loss. If this is true, the coach might then ask, "What would be most helpful for you today?" or, "What are your options?" If he will give himself permission to "window shop" a bit and explore new options around vocation and passions, he could experience an internal shift. He is still looking but eager to *move from wandering to walking*.

Reflect on:
Am I avoiding the inevitable?

Often the same life lessons keep coming our way until we have learned that particular lesson and are ready to move on toward higher self-actualization and deeper spiritual maturity.

Coaching Discoveries for Transformation

As individuals are working on their desired changes in life, it is important for them to define and articulate exactly what is keeping them stuck. In other words: What are the barriers that need to be labeled, understood, and removed for one to have movement forward and ignite one's true potential?

Denial keeps our false self strong and alive.

A coaching model that might help is Timothy Gallwey's Realizing Potential model:

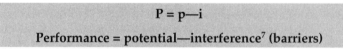

$$P = p—i$$

Performance = potential—interference[7] (barriers)

When using Gallwey's model, it is often best to work from the end to the beginning. In other words, consider first the interference and how it might be keeping one from reaching his or her potential. When that interference is lessened, performance is increased.

The things causing the interference are barriers to the desired outcome the person being coached is seeking.

The coach needs to listen for barriers. Barriers could manifest as a false belief system, attitude, or saboteur. It could be someone's voice that the client keeps hearing that is saying the person is not good enough, smart enough, or adventurous enough. It could be fear. Shame. Addiction. Learning to unlearn the things that are keeping us stuck and relearning new ways that are good for us, ways that push us forward to a better place, can be extremely challenging. It is usually the internal blocks (i.e., personal thoughts and emotions) that are attracting the external unhealthy blocks (i.e., the expressions of old patterns). Denial can be a coping mechanism for all of us at certain times in our lives, but is not meant to be used long-term. It only keeps us stuck, because we are not allowing the truth to enter in and birth our true self. Secrets, hiding things, and denial can be powerful blocks to one's forward movement. Denial keeps our false self strong and alive. Our false self does not want us to acknowledge our blocks, much less remove them and start using healthier coping skills and enter an authentic life. These internal issues often need an external objective person who is willing to mirror them for the Person Being Coached (PBC). Who needs to know about these struggles so they might be trusted enough to walk with you through the ripples from pain to purpose?

Clarifying BARRIERS

The following *BARRIERS* acrostic is a helpful and easy way to help you as a leader and/or coach to navigate individuals from being stuck to unstuck.

> **Coach around BARRIERS**
> Bullet-proof (stubborness)
> Avoidance
> Resistance
> Roadblocks
> Impulse
> Ego
> Resentment
> Sabotage

Coach Around
BARRIERS
Bullet-proof
(stubborness)
Avoidance
Resistance
Roadblocks
Impulse
Ego
Resentment
Sabotage

B—Bullet-proof (stubborness)

(Remember that the Ripple model framework suggests lack of clarity/self-awareness, unwillingness to face the unfamiliar, and moving from denial might be areas in which to do some coaching.)

Difficult times test our character, determination, and willingness to change and become better. Moving forward toward health, wholeness, happiness, and better decision-making requires us to look at what is keeping us stuck. One may reflect on these questions:

> *What is in the way?*
>
> *What is blocking your path?*
>
> *Is it something external, like a huge boulder in the road?*
>
> *Or is it something internal that is blocking your growth?*

A—Avoidance

To illustrate avoidance and moving from pain to purpose, let me share this experience with you.

I (Randy) had a conversation with a dear friend one day. As we were talking she said, "How did I get here? What have I done to get me to this place?"

I asked her what she meant and what was going on. She had recently broken up with her boyfriend again. She believes that they do not have a future together. They have had an off/on relationship for years and have really had a difficult time cutting the ties. So, she has acknowledged that here she is again in a situation that she has been in before; the pain of getting out and leaving the old is extremely difficult. The fear of being alone is overwhelming, and the fear of thinking of the dating world again and meeting new people, starting all over, is even more frightening and depressing.

We all seem to want to jump past the pain of the breakup and simply get into a new relationship where the euphoria and newness fills us up with joy and connection. But my friend said she is smarter now and has a bit more understanding of her decisions. She is beginning to notice some trends in the characteristics and qualities of the guys she typically dates and appears to be attracted to. Looking into her heart and inner self is scary for her because she said, "I am afraid of what I am going to find."

I understand. We talked about that a bit, but not too much. She was getting to the point where she did not want to talk about it anymore. Feelings and fears were starting to surface. We all need time to explore, digest, reflect, uncover, change, and then act on our new learnings to break those unhealthy blocks that keep us stuck or attracting people that are unhealthy for us. I encouraged her to keep searching and to not be afraid at looking internally. *My experience is that this cannot be done alone because we need the objectivity and trust of others. We also need a safe environment to do this important work. In a coaching conversation you might want to explore:*

- How do you know if a relationship should be terminated?
- How will you know if new healthy boundaries can be set?
- What is preventing you from leaving a relationship?

We need time to explore, digest, reflect, uncover, change, and then act on our new learnings.

We also need a safe environment to do this important work.

- What is preventing you from leaving a job that you have acknowledged as being a block in your life?

R—Resistance

Our resistance can be certain circumstances, viewpoints, and/or fear of change. Perhaps we can learn lessons around our judgments, opinions, and abilities or inabilities to accept the diversities in today's world. Resistance is more emotional. For example, have you ever met someone who always has to be right? They must always win. It becomes a struggle for power. If they lose or don't get their way, they get upset and irritable. We all know that no one is right 100 percent of the time. Coaching is a powerful tool to move persons through their resistance.

Coaches may ask:

Coaching is a powerful tool to move persons through their resistance.

- What are your barriers that keep you in pain?
- What are you afraid of?
- What are you ashamed of?
- What are your triggers that set you off?

What makes your defense system kick in so that you become "resistant"? This is usually a clear sign that this is the area that needs exploration and focus.

Unhealthy impulses cause us to say and do things that we regret.

R—Road Blocks

Our blocks that keep us stuck could be people. Blocks could also be places, circumstances, and/or things. A coach might ask:

- What is pulling you backward and keeping you stuck?
- Who is holding you back, not wanting you to change? Why?
- What support do you have around you that nurtures the new dreams?

I—Impulse

"Impulse" is defined by Dictionary.com as

A sudden wish or urge that prompts an unpremeditated act or feeling; an abrupt inclination. A motivating force or tendency: *"Respect for the liberty of others is not a natural impulse in most men."*—Bertrand Russell from Dictionary.com.[8]

Unhealthy impulses cause us to say and do things that we regret and wish we could take back. Slowing down and taking time to work on ourselves is challenging at best. A good coach needs to be fully present with clients and even mirror their energy or offer challenges to them that might go against their norm to create space for them to think, feel, or learn. Here is such a case where a person who is impulsive needs the coach to challenge her to stop—at least slow down and reflect. I just had a client thank me the other day for our time on the phone. I asked her what she meant by her statement. She stated that in her hectic life she looked forward to the time on the phone with me to slow down and get to the core of life. She stated her coaching time served as a sacred place and time to block out the noise of life and hear the spirit of her inner voice.

Some reflective questions a coach may want to ask an impulsive person include:

What do I hear when I'm quiet?

What's going on in the stillness?

What keeps me busy?

E—Ego

Wayne Dyer is an inspirational writer and speaker that I (Randy) follow. He once said that the ego is simply "Edging God Out."[10]

Ego feeds the false self. It does not want to be wrong. Ego often feeds our greed and materialistic attitudes. Oftentimes our false self has no logic or rational thinking. Our false self is our aberrant behavior, addictions, and dysfunctions that lead us to pain and unfulfillment. The false self wants to keep you stuck, unhappy, and away from your true calling and destiny. The false self will win unless we realize these are blocks that keep us from our true self. These blocks can be broken down and defeated by understanding the thoughts and feelings that take us to these behaviors in the first place.

Consider these coaching questions:

- Where are some places you currently go that feed your false self?
- What things, people, or substances are you addicted to?
- What causes you to follow these behaviors that eventually bring pain?
- What behaviors bring you the most joy?

Sidebar notes:

Ego is simply "edging God out."[9]

Resentment is a barrier that manifests in our attitudes, belief system, and unresolved feelings and emotions.

Getting to the truth, being 100 percent honest, is very difficult and something that few of us do.

R—Resentment

Resentment is a barrier that manifests in our attitudes, belief systems, and unresolved feelings and emotions. Resentment is usually intentional. However, for many persons resentment is an emotional block that they use as an unhealthy coping skill. Many are in denial around resentment issues, so resentment remains quite intentional, though many are not conscious of their own behavior. One of the most interesting lessons I (Randy) have learned about my own blocks and triggers is that so many of mine were relational and wrapped around feelings, emotions, and a false belief system. Resentment and anger really did some work on me. Resentment is a big trigger for me. Resentment takes away all gratitude. Under my resentment were layers of hurt, betrayal, and grief. Resentment was my "I'll show them!" attitude and behavior. Anger can be a wonderful motivator to move forward, but resentment can be extremely ugly. We all know some folks that could use a good anger management course. Anger hurts others. Resentment simply hurts yourself.

Coaching assignments such as the following will often provide fuel to the client's agenda.

> Will you accept this challenge? Make a list of your barriers and toxins that feed your false self.

S—Sabotage

Getting to the truth and being 100 percent honest is very difficult and something that few do. We are only as good as our word. We, unfortunately, for the most part are looking for a quick fix or a band-aid to a difficult problem. Most of us are unwilling to do the depth of work required to let our true self shine and deaden our false self that is the saboteur. Pain and certain crises in life, whether relational, professional, personal, or academic, can be used to get our attention and push us toward healthy or unhealthy behaviors. The decision to which way we go is up to one's clarity and understanding of self. We are at times our own worst enemy. The false self wants nothing more than to defeat the true self and thus rob us of the destiny for which we were created.

This is the tough process that requires a lot of reflection and self-evaluation, but is part of being a spiritual traveler (one who has spiritual thirsts but not necessarily formal connections with an institutional church or religion). This individual journey makes us a bit different. Blocks and barriers have to be removed. To remove them, they must be understood. You must understand why and how the aberrant behavior got there in the first place. This moral

Resentment simply hurts yourself.

We are at times our own worst enemy.

Spiritual Traveler: one who has spiritual thirsts but not necessarily formal connections with an institutional church or religion self-inventory will require complete honesty and confession. It is okay to start this on your own, but I (Randy) learned that it takes the honesty and objectivity of others (a good coach) because at times we are not able to see ourselves and situations clearly through our own judgment and discernment.

Coaching questions to consider:

> How will you know if you are ready to do this work?

- How will you know if you are ready to do this work?
- What will move you through your fears?
- What are the benefits of uncovering your true self and moving into your destiny?

Before we go into the Seven Keys, here are some things we want you to remember to be an effective coach:

> Whatever the issues may be, moving from pain to purpose requires greater self-awareness and clarity.

1. Entry points for your coaching conversations will be different—meet the PBC (Person Being Coached) where the client is, not where you want him or her to be. Start where the client wants to start.
2. Make the client work hard to find his or her own self-discovery.
3. The PBC sets the agenda.
4. The PBC takes the initiative.
5. The conversations are about honesty and action; don't let the client ramble and "beat around the bush."
6. Coach the PBC through his or her barriers.
7. Coach the client to identify and move blocks.
8. Find the coachable moments (remember this brings the harmony to life!).
9. Listen for disconnects and blind spots—what is not being said.
10. Encourage and celebrate learnings/landmarks.
11. Create trust and hope. Open-ended questions create hope.

Applying the Seven Key Questions to Individuals

Another way of experiencing transformation with a client is to utilize the seven key questions as a way of helping the client explore needed shifts.

The coach can listen for possible needed shifts about which the client may or may not be clear. Most people are moving from pain to purpose after the heart-wrenching realization that things are not the way they want them to be. In an individual's life, this could involve facing the brutal realities around relationships that need to change or be terminated, family dysfunctions, unhappiness at work, etc. For a group or organization, this could be loss of revenues, employee retention problems, lack of productivity, etc. Whatever the issues may be, moving from pain to purpose requires greater self-awareness and clarity. Often, things, beliefs, and ideas need to shift. At times, old ways of thinking must change into entirely new learnings and discoveries. How long this takes depends on our pain threshold, our depth of denial, our openness to change, and our willingness to accept the truth.

Since you are trying to get a handle on the coach approach, here's a possible application of the coach approach using the first key question. Remember you are not, nor are you expected to be, a therapist who untangles emotions or the past. You are a coach seeking to move the coachable individual forward. If the PBC is not ready to go forward, refer that person to a counselor or therapist. So, for review and application, consider these clues for coaching individuals.

For forward movement to occur, the client must show openness to change and willingness to shift. Often times if the person is bulletproof, more dialogue is needed. Time away for deeper thought and reflection may be required, or additional time may be needed to allow the person the sacred time needed for digestion and processing. Big life changes and shifts have a major impact on our souls as we try our best to navigate to live our destiny and tap into our true callings. At best, this is messy! In our experience it is very messy, but the Spirit and soul work is most alive and effective in the activity and collaboration for change.

As one's openness begins to unfold, one can begin to gently move beyond denial. As denial loosens its grip, some will become much more interested and willing to invest in change and explore options for new solutions.

Possible coaching questions for jump-starting a coaching conversation might include:

- What needs to happen today?
- What will help make that happen?
- What will you do if this does not happen today?

Key Question 1: What are the needed shifts?

The first key—What shifts are needed now?—is important and may have different entry points in the Ripple diagram based on the person's goals and understanding where the person being coached (PBC) currently is. If the PBC appears to have good self-awareness and clarity, the process may quickly advance from the inner ripple of the chart. If the person simply states that he or she feels stuck and has no idea where to go next, the coach will spend as much time as needed to gain clarity in regards to where

> Remember that you are not, nor are you expected to be, a therapist who untangles emotions or the past. You are a coach seeking to move the coachable individual forward.

> For forward movement to occur, the client must show openness to change and willingness to shift.

> Key 1
> What are the shifts needed? Now?

the PBC is now and where he or she wants to go. For example, a client may state, "I hate my job. It is so painful to wake up in the morning, get dressed and get into the office. My job drains me. I want to find greater purpose, and explore what is my true calling in life." This kind of statement and realization is fertile soil to begin an exciting coaching conversation.

In this particular example, the shifts are fairly clear—the person being coached might simply not understand the need for the shifts in the first place. Or it could be the client wants change around job and fulfillment in his or her work life. This realization is great and is to be celebrated, but can create a tremendous amount of stress. It is natural for someone to want to change jobs and/or careers, but many of us will start making excuses to stay stuck. Some declare, "I have had this job a long time and feel very comfortable here." Often, that is not a reason to stay, but a reason to move on and shake things up a bit.

Another consideration: today's work climate may demand external shifts so the client may find it may not be so much about internal shifts in the beginning. With downsizing and the increase in the number of pink slips, one's pain can easily be job termination from cutbacks. Later you will note that key question 3 is important because our decisions will have an effect on those around us. Shifts may be about your family system, friends, and/or colleagues. You will want to help the person being coached explore all areas. The Ripple model can help you coach through the PBC's questions/issues and move the person forward with these seven key, or other, appropriate coaching questions.

As the initial conversations begin, you will quickly begin to realize that change is needed. Things simply cannot stay the way they are. This insight is a big first step, but many will get stuck at this early starting point. After the realization that change is needed, one must then begin to look at the next steps. The next steps will be very unfamiliar. The old way is not working. All the PBC knows is the old way. Looking at options for a new way will be un-nerving and create uneasiness. Facing the unfamiliar cannot be done alone. Alone, people will simply slip quickly back into the old ways and will lose objectivity toward movement forward.

Coaching questions may include:

- What is really going on?
- What are the pinches here?
- What are the resources needed to move forward?

As you begin to embrace these questions and, more importantly, begin to embrace some honest answers, two things may happen:

Big life changes and shifts have a major impact on our soul as we live our destiny and tap into our true callings.

Openness to new learnings and stepping beyond one's denial and fears play a key part in birthing the new.

- Openness to change and shifts, or
- Person shuts down, becomes defensive.

Key Question 2: What are the shifts about anyway?

Question 2 (What are the shifts about anyway?) helps the individual explore and face unfamiliar landscapes that will be uncomfortable and tiring in the beginning. Openness to new learnings and stepping beyond one's denial and fears play key parts in birthing the new. As one pushes through the unfamiliar, momentum, clarity and collaboration from others will increase. The next issue for many then is the loneliness they feel when it comes to moving forward with new behaviors or attitudes. Or they may fear failure as they embark upon new horizons of life and career. Then the coach might ask questions related to key question 3.

Key 2
What are the shifts about anyway?

Key Question 3: Who needs to know about the shifts?

This begins to introduce and utilize the coach approach to a deeper level as you move beyond the first two questions. Our true self (the person we are created to be) loves us, and nurtures us and others. Our true self has the freedom and confidence to dance in front of the mirror, show vulnerability, and have an open mind and an open heart. Our true self does not sabotage our future. Our true self demonstrates mind, body, and soul integration. Our true self has head and heart integration. Our true self is not self-absorbed and short-focused. Keeping our true self strong requires great intention and dedication. One of the best questions I have ever been asked by a coach is, "Who can you stand beside who allows you to be your very best?" Great question. I think of this often. At times, others' personal agendas and motives can get in the way of one's passion and success. We need to know who the persons are who can propel us forward to our hopes, dreams, and goals. Who are the persons who can help us overcome our blind spots and challenges. Who is the person(s) who plays the role of "tough love" in your life, offering much needed truth-telling?

These internal issues often need an external person(s) who is willing to mirror them for the person being coached. Who needs to know about these struggles so they might be trusted enough to walk with you through the ripples from pain to purpose? The forward movement comes when the person being coached can respond and embrace the following questions:

Key 3
Who needs to know about the shifts?

- Our true self does not sabotage our future.
- Our true self demonstrates mind, body, and soul integration.
- Our true self has head and heart integration.
- Our true self is not self-absorbed and short-focused.
- Keeping our true self strong requires great intention and dedication.

- Who can help you move forward?
- Who can help you walk into the unfamiliar?
- Who can help you explore new options and create new discoveries?

Key Question 4: What about the dissenters/skeptics?

Key 4
What do the
dissenters/skeptics
need to know?

In many instances internal voices seek to sidetrack or sabotage the shifts. Or it may be those persons you hang around who seek to sidetrack you from being all you are created to be. They also can be people who clearly do not understand the change and transitions you are trying to make. Sometimes they are not intentionally trying to stop you. Other times they are so they can remain in their comfort zone or preserve their personal agendas or control you.

- What's keeping you stuck?
- Who is keeping you stuck?
- What advantage do you gain from sticking around these people?
- What would happen if you jettisoned these people from your life?

Key Question 5: What timing is needed?

Key 5
What timing is needed
in making these
shifts?

The element of timing has to do with the coach and the person being coached. Here the coach looks for the coachable moments when the PBC is ripe for good coaching around a particular shift.

I love music and there are many songs about life being a journey and not a final destination. A good coach listens to discern where the PBC is along his or her own unique journey, honoring the process—being imperfect and accepting that this is part of the human condition.

We must accept that this is a journey—a life that will have failed relationships, career transitions, great losses, but also great victories and accomplishments. Living by the lessons learned moves us to greater understanding, clarity, freedom, and fulfillment. Transformation is fueled from living by our lessons learned. When we know better and have truly embraced our changes and transitions, authentic transformation is birthed.

Coaching questions to consider:

- Where are you in your journey?
- Where do you want to be in six months? A year?
- What is the next step you are willing to take now?
- On a scale of 1 (unfulfilled) to 10 (very fulfilled) how would you describe where you are now?

Key Question 6: Who can help us move forward now?

At times people are very clearly blocks that keep us stagnant. At other times the blocks can be much more subtle. It is important to know and embrace those who can move us forward. Peer pressure, at any age, is extremely strong in our world today. Children are being pressured into sex, drugs, and unhealthy behavior at alarmingly younger and younger ages.

Who are the cheerleaders for your new dream? This powerful question can help you discover who can help you move forward and discern negative peer pressure that pulls one backward.

People blocking our true self can be the abusive caretakers in our lives. The abusive father or mother in a family system can cause a great deal of harm to one's self-confidence and self-esteem. This can be physical abuse, verbal abuse, emotional abuse, passive-aggressive behavior, etc. Many of us have unresolved blocks that allow the cycle of dysfunction to be passed on and on throughout our family systems from grandparent, to parent, to child, and to grandchild. These issues then trickle into our places of work, creating a new level of dysfunction in the workplace with our teams and committees. For true authentic change, the cycle must stop somewhere. Our blocks, toxins, and unhealthy coping skills are learned behaviors. They simply manifest in all of us in different ways. We all have our "Achilles heel" in life and need to deal with it. This helps to keep us humble. I admire the saying I once saw on a T-shirt in Boston—"Be humble or be humbled!" Humility and surrender are important spiritual lessons in life that should be integrated into all areas of our lives. Humility and surrender keeps our compassion alive. Soulful leaders have the discernment of compassion for building bridges and understand that judgment builds barriers.

Acknowledging that certain people and/or relationships may be barriers for you can be extremely painful. We have all heard of extremely sad stories in which the abused daughter will not admit that her mother or father is being abusive. The daughter cannot imagine telling someone what is really happening, for these are her parents who love her. They don't really mean to do the horrible things that they do. We hear these conversations all the time in the coffee shop, the grocery store, the dog park, and on television. We have also heard these statements around married couples and people dating, "Why does she stay with him? He treats her so badly. Why can't she see that he cheats on her and really doesn't love her? She would be so much better off if she could leave him."

Sometimes those who can help are authors of books who share similar journeys with you. One of my favorites is Terence Gorski. He states:

Key 6
Who can help us move forward now?

We all have our "Achilles heel" in life and need to deal with it.

Humility and surrender are important spiritual lessons that should be integrated into all areas of our lives.

If you came from a dysfunctional family, there are two very good reasons you may have trouble getting love right. The first is that dysfunctional relationships are contagious: Children catch them from their parents because they learn by doing what their parents do. If your parents were practitioners of destructive intimacy, that is all they were able to teach you... The second reason you are liable to have relationship problems is that dysfunctional families fail to provide their children with emotional, intellectual, and communication skills necessary to conduct healthy relationships. How can you drive a car safely without learning driving skills? You can't.[11]

Humility and surrender keep our compassion alive.

Coaching around these issues can be effective if the person is ready to move forward and be coached. The coaching readiness factor must be assessed. *If the person is not able to move forward and appears tangled in his or her past, this is a good sign that counseling is really needed around these delicate issues, and not coaching.* Jane Creswell states:

The primary difference between coaching and other types of personal help is again related to who is viewed as the expert. Just as in athletic coaching, in mentoring, consulting, and counseling, the person offering the service is clearly the expert. In business coaching the PBC is the expert. The coach is simply a guide to help the PBC keep growing, reaching goals, and achieving his or her potential.[12]

(Current research is suggesting that personal therapy and coaching really complement each other. Coaching is being used as a powerful tool in some therapeutic sessions now with clinical professionals such as is presented at http://harvardcoaching. org/ with McLean Hospital and Harvard Medical School in Massachusetts.)

Coaching questions to consider:

- Who are the people in your life who erode your self-esteem and self-confidence?
- How do they prevent you from moving forward?
- What things are you willing to give up to move forward?
- What are you not willing to give up no matter the degree of pain these things, or people, cause?
- Who can move you forward?

For some the process of owning who keeps you stuck is essential in raising their awareness and encouraging them to open doors for those who can move them forward.

Key Question 7: What is next?

For me (Randy), "Taking off my tap shoes" was a next step. This is a phrase that I have used for years. I have never taken a dance class, nor do I own a pair of tap shoes, but I love all kinds of dance and think of the image of professional tap dancers performing. They can really move at times, tapping faster and faster and faster. It is exhilarating to watch! This can be symbolic of my life, and I am certain many others can relate to it as well as we continue to be stuck in the cycle of our business and busyness. When do we have time to truly be alone to reflect? Then, after a great amount of reflection, we still need to move into action to change things that need to be changed. And, this takes more time! But, to experience true transformation you've got to "take off those tap shoes," slow down, and be fully present.

Ingrid Bacci says, "If you are afraid of being alone, you are dependent on others for your sense of self, and if you are dependent on others, you block your receptivity to inner guidance. Being willing to be alone involves being willing to be different, to have commitments and values that don't blend with any crowd."[13]

Staying busy was a barrier and coping mechanism for me. To stay so busy never left me any time to look at myself and even begin to face my demons. This kept me in the cycle of quick knee-jerk reactions with little or no thought to my problems, which in return put me in many uncomfortable situations. I can remember the first time I got home and did not turn on the TV, radio, or computer. I challenged myself to simply put everything down: the briefcase, the laptop, the cell phone, and the bundle of mail/bills. I sat on my couch and wanted to sit quietly for fifteen minutes. I could not do it! My heart was racing, and my anxiety was building by the second. I had so many things I needed to do: bills to pay, people to call, a workout at the gym, etc. All things that truly could wait.

The first time I attempted to have my "down time," I made it about ten minutes before I jumped up, turned on the TV and computer, and jumped back into my life. Oh, the relief of being busy and getting back on the treadmill of my busyness to run from my problems and issues. As we continue to hide behind our unhealthy coping skills, our internal longing for clarity and our hunger for greater peace and purpose keep tugging at us. They will tug more and more until they get our attention. I don't think I fit the category of a true workaholic because my busyness could be centered around any project, not just work.

Key 7
What is next?

To experience transformation you have to take off your "tap shoes."

Gary Zukav states:

The pains and distresses and violences that you experience can be considered as signposts along the path that you have chosen. If you have chosen the path of learning through jealousy, for example, you will experience anxiety and fear of loss of what you think you cannot live without because these experiences are part of the path of learning through jealousy. If you choose the path of learning through anger, you will experience rejection and violence; if you choose the path of love, you will experience being loved by others, and so on, because the choice of a particular path is also the choice of particular types of experiences.[14]

Soulful leaders have the discernment of compassion for building bridges and they understand that judgment builds barriers.

Coaching questions to consider:

- How do you make time for more "down time"?
- What scares you about having time alone?
- What emotions surface while you sit in silence?
- What do you hear in your silence?
- What happens when the activity/noise stops?
- What are your next steps?

As a coach, consider where you and the person(s) you are coaching are in the Ripple model. Think about how the BARRIERS acrostic applies to your life. Ask yourself and the PBC (person being coached) the seven key questions. When you're dealing with people who are going through the calm or overwhelming waves of change, remember the models, assessments, and questions. These questions become tools of transformation in times of change and transition—also known as life!

Making Shifts That Matter in Institutions and Organizations

What do you do when an organizational system repeatedly discovers many disconnects between respective missions, personnel and supervision policies, and values? When these storms gather regularly and the fallout from the stresses encountered drain energy, challenge values and next steps, and consume personnel with "fighting internal battles" rather than "pursuing their mission and destiny," what's a leader to do?

Such an experience was the reality we were invited into as coaches on a particular occasion. We clarified the storm, tested reality against perceptions, and got clear about their desired outcomes for our coaching relationship. The Ripple model proved to be a powerful guide for our coaching relationship.

Ripple Model a Powerful Guide
Moving Beyond Denial and Facing Reality

This proves a tough task to face under the best of circumstances, but when stress is eating away at the health of those in the organization and constant challenges become increasingly combative, the coach approach creates a climate for the leaders and organization caught in this pinch to face realities and move forward. This approach also gave this particular group permission to have this dialogue about the new shifts needed to enter into the future changes.

Dimensions of the Ripple Model:

- Moving beyond Denial/Facing New Reality
- Openness to Change/Shifts
- Facing the Unfamiliar
- Self-Awareness/Clarity
- Forward Movement Brings Clarity and Momentum
- Commitment to Forward Movement Builds Community and Collaboration

New dreams could not have been seen until they were willing to step outside their comfort zones.

Openness to Change/Shifts

This is critical for any person or organization caught in a storm. If you're not willing to change and move beyond the comfort zones and familiarity, change is not likely to happen and new dreams will not likely be birthed. The coach approach really helped this group explore what the future might look like if...? This coaching exercise began to help them count the cost of change, but also began to create possibilities in their minds. New dreams could not have been seen until they were willing to step outside their comfort zones.

Facing the Unfamiliar

This task takes time and patience when exploring the "what else's?" of life and work. What will it take to move into the new? Since many of those in this organization were women, they began to use the image of pregnancy. So, as good coaches, we picked up on that metaphor and began to help them explore questions such as: "What new is inside of you?" "What is it like to be spiritually pregnant?" "What will the new birth call forth in you?" These and many other coaching experiences proved to birth excitement, new skill set training, and dialogue with other organizations that have moved through organizational and funding shifts.

Self-Awareness/Clarity

Coming to grips with reality, new possibilities, new dreams, and new skills can and often does provide the momentum to move on and believe that "you can do it!" Questions about what you say yes to and no to became powerful aids in helping them get clear and focused. Saying no truly becomes a grief and loss experience for persons and must be acknowledged before the group is able to move on.

Forward Movement Brings Clarity and Momentum

This "can do" attitude, the broadening and deepening vision and landscape for business creates, and typically sustains, the momentum and helps clarify the new vision. Coaching pulls this out of folks, builds ownership of the new dream, and provides the encouragement to keep moving. A great coaching question emerged from the group as they discussed, "What makes your baby kick?"

Commitment to Forward Movement, Collaboration/Community

Once the new vision, skills, and momentum begin, it becomes a matter of commitment and community. The coach approach provides a great lens to help the group see connections in dreams, values, and intent. This builds community that sustains the dream and moves the group forward. Again, this is not easy, but the coach approach makes it happen and provides the trusted, objective companionship for those dark storms that may still come, but the new dreams and new skills allow you to pass *through* the storm rather than get *stuck in* the storm!

The power of the Ripple model is that it brings clarity to the multiple issues and often multiple layers involved in making organizational shifts, unlocking the future while managing the present and presence of an organization and staff.

Changing the Future, Preserving the Treasures

Today's rapidly changing culture has brought forth a deteriorating interest in the treasures of the church culture or even attending church. Today's churches or other organizations cannot avoid change. Some can deal with incremental change and survive and maybe even thrive. Most are in situations calling for systemic and radical change. For instance, many churches are filled with dedicated senior adults who staff programs, give tithes, and design ministries. Similarly, many corporations have many tenured employees wanting to know what to do next. Increasingly, the younger generation, particularly those who haven't grown up in church families, are not even thinking about church in their weekly activities. What's a church to do? How are pastors and churches to respond to the growing apathy of the culture while preserving those who are in the current membership and leadership pool? How can a church or any organization make shifts without creating unnecessary waves of discontent?

What new is inside them?

What is it like to be spiritually pregnant?

What will the new birth call forth in them?

Many businesses and nonprofit organizations are suffering in today's struggling economy. Tough decisions are being made daily and sometimes hourly that will impact many families and communities across the country. How do leaders in these critical times manage the present while they birth the future? How can organizations honor the workers' contributions over the years while at the same time face the economic realities of the business? These are truly challenges that are real. It is our conviction that soulful leaders can minimize the destructive waves, even in these tough realities, by utilizing the Ripple model and soulful leader perspectives and values.

Saying no truly becomes a grief and loss experience for persons and must be acknowledged before the group is able to move on.

Soulful leadership, whether you are dealing with families, individuals, churches, or businesses, seeks to listen to those involved, discern collaboratively next steps for the organization, and enlist the energies and resources of others to make the new dream and next steps become a reality. Research tells us that if you can get about 25 to 30 percent to buy into a new idea, they can lead a culture shift in any organization. So often the easiest groups to engage are those who are newcomers to the church and those who have children or grandchildren who are still in the community at large but are mostly inactive in the church. The newcomers can help create a new value and leadership model from the time they enter the fellowship. The other folks are looking for something meaningful that works to reach their loved ones. For church leaders, we truly believe that God has a remnant in the Church that sees the future and, if led, are willing to help fund and create that dream. (This remnant is also discussed in *Spiritual Leadership in a Secular Age* [Chalice Press, 2005] and *Reaching People Under 40 While Keeping People Over 60* [Chalice Press, 2007], and at www.transformingsolutions.org .)

Coaching is a powerful tool to make this happen in a timely, efficient, and effective manner that honors the values of the past and co-creates an agenda that will move leaders, organizations and dreams forward.

We have previously discussed the use of the coaching model when working with individuals. Chapter 5 describes the Ripple model and the BARRIER model, allowing you to see how coaching individuals can begin with their story and their awareness or the lack thereof. While these same models and approaches might also be feasible and effective working with organizations, chapter 6 is written around the seven key questions and coaching tools for building BRIDGES between members of the organization or group faced with change. Understand that all models and approaches are possible tools for working in some or all situations. Determining the best model and approach for a given coaching relationship depends on the coach's skill and the client's openness and learning style. Working with teams, groups, organizations, businesses, churches, or judicatories calls for basically the same skill set and often uses some of the same principles and models we have introduced previously. However, some significant distinctives must be considered and incorporated into effectively coaching more than one person.

Distinctives to Remember When Coaching Organizations

Coaching a group or organization utilizes the basics of coaching along with another level of skills including these:

> - Listening at deeper levels to hear even what is not being said and paying attention to more than one person at a time.
> - Inviting the group to establish their own ground rules for the coaching session. What is needed to insure effective decision making from this organization now? What are the non-negotiables for this discussion?
> - Insuring that all voices "at the table" are heard.
> - Finding and keeping focus for the organization and leadership team.
> - Honoring the values of the organization the group wants to preserve and what the members need to let go of to be more effective in their marketplace.

Determining the best model and approach for a given coaching relationship depends on the coach's skill and the client's openness and learning style.

What are the non-negotiables for this discussion?

Create win/win scenarios whenever possible.

- Honoring confidentiality as you work with the group as a whole or individuals in the group.
- Co-creating consensus through coaching.
- Capturing the data from the group's dialogue around the seven keys so the group/organization can then see and make decisions. The group selects a recorder to capture the thoughts.
- Creating win/win scenarios whenever possible.
- Honoring different learning and communications styles of the group (i.e., some need visuals, others need dialogue, others need processing/reflective times).
- Remembering that coaching can require linear, cyclical, or random approaches depending on the learning or work style of the group.

Most organizations—whether profit or nonprofit—face changes on almost a daily basis. Many organizations wrestle to preserve heritage and values while customizing services to meet the needs and wishes of a changing demographic, economic base, cultural system, etc. Staying relevant, flexible, and real in a rapidly changing culture is a challenge for any organization. Coaching can and does help leaders and organizations customize and contextualize services. Coaches who work with organizations understand the ingredients of creating a coaching culture and the power of assessing readiness and coachability. Without readiness and openness to change no person or organization can experience healthy and transformational change.

Without readiness and openness to change no person or organization can experience healthy transformation.

Let's toss another pebble of change into the waters and look at a way of making shifts without making waves in organizations and institutions. This model applies to organizations of any size or purpose.

First, how do you know that an organization or institution is coachable?

Assessing Coachability

First, how do you know that an organization or institution is coachable? This is a key question. Some organizations want a quick fix to a challenge. In reality, they need the expertise of a consultant. Here are some indicators that an organization will respond well to a coach approach to introducing and managing change:

- The leadership team that makes decisions is open to challenge, open to change, and eager to work with others to make it happen.
- Organizational members or employees are open to challenge, open to stretching, open to change (stepping outside their personal comfort zones), and eager to work with each other to make change happen. Remember, the shifts start inside people first! For instance, in corporations all over the country, more managers

and supervisors are having more one-on-one, face-to-face conversations and less e-mail dialogue. Building relationships and being sensitive to personal and professional needs empowers organizations to develop and retain their best assets—employees.

- Core values of the organization are understood by key leadership, or they have a willingness to define them.
- Willingness exists to expend energy to discover next steps and how each leader and member or employee can work to move the organization forward.
- Members exhibit an openness to collaboration with others and willingness to hear all sides of an issue before making a decision.
- Members exhibit an openness to establishing a time line to implement whatever changes are discovered and decided upon.
- Key issues of coaching are likely to include, but are not limited to, the seven key questions.

Effective shifts most often occur from the inside out.

Other distinctives of working with organizations involve work with teams. Patrick Lencioni provides great insights for coaches seeking to identify the nature of the team they are invited to coach. Lencioni's model is built around identifying the five dysfunctions of a team:

1. Absence of trust
2. Fear of conflict
3. Lack of commitment
4. Avoidance of accountability
5. Inattention to results[1]

He goes on to provide indicators the coach should look and listen for that might suggest members of a team are exhibiting one or more of the dysfunctions.[2] Lencioni also provides a very helpful self-assessment that the team can use to self-assess their health or dysfunction.[3]

Coaching a group, organization, or team brings unique challenges, especially when you discover dysfunctional behavior obviously blocking any advancement.[4] This calls on you to exercise great insight and dedication to the truth, not to what the team wants to hear. You will need to:

- Observe the team and determine the dysfunction that seems to be holding up the team most. Ask questions in the coaching conversation that will help the members discover their dysfunction and shed light on the actions they need to take to improve their team dynamics (i.e., if you see lack of trust, ask: How often do you admit mistakes to each other? What would have to happen for you to feel safe admitting mistakes with your team?).[5]

> • Keep in mind that the framework in the Ripple model includes: openness to change, facing reality, increasing awareness, learning to face the unfamiliar, a mutual commitment to forward movement and community, and embracing forward movement that will create clarity and momentum. Learning to hear or observe these issues becomes critical for creating waves of hope among the ripples of change.

Now let's explore each area from a coach approach as the pebble of change hits the pond that ripples through an organization.

Ripple Model for Coaching Organizations

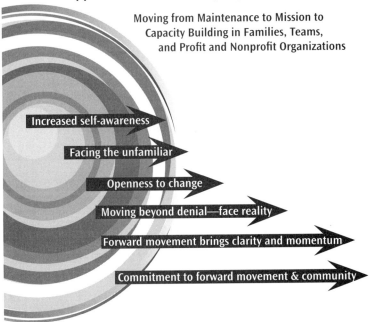

Moving from Maintenance to Mission to Capacity Building in Families, Teams, and Profit and Nonprofit Organizations

Increased self-awareness

Facing the unfamiliar

Openness to change

Moving beyond denial—face reality

Forward movement brings clarity and momentum

Commitment to forward movement & community

Often you have to change the behaviors, and then the feelings will follow.

Possible Shifts and How to Make Them Happen

Seven Keys for Making Shifts without Making Waves

1. What are the shifts needed? (and which are needed right now?)
2. What are the shifts about anyway?
3. Who needs to know about the shifts?
4. What about the dissenters/skeptics?
5. What timing is needed?
6. Who can help us move forward now?
7. What is next?

> **Framework for Using the Ripple Model**
> - People and organizations enter shifts from a variety of entry points and perspectives on life
> - Following the ripples from inward to outward focus offers a pathway to progress
> - Different groupings/affinity groups follow essentially the same steps moving forward
>   - ~ Self awareness/clarity
>   - ~ Facing the unfamiliar
>   - ~ Openness to change/shifts
>   - ~ Moving beyond denial
>   - ~ Forward movement brings clarity and momentum
>   - ~ Commitment to forward movement and collaboration
> - Effective shifts most often occur from the inside out
> - HARMONY model (see appendices) provides powerful coaching questions that move persons/organizations forward regardless of where they might be when the coaching relationship begins
> - Progress occurs as persons/organizations move forward from a purely self-focused perspective to an outward focused perspective
> - Often you have to change the behaviors and then the feelings will follow
> - Clarifying limiting beliefs is often part of moving forward
> - Coaching is about discovering that which is already within and bringing it into light
>
> Adaptation of the Engles Scale

- Clarifying limiting beliefs is often part of moving forward.
- Coaching is about discovering that which is already within and bringing it to light.
- Discoveries are most often made in community rather than in isolation.

Let's look at a coaching scenario that's representative of the type of change issues faced by many organizations. A personnel search committee calls for coaching as they begin their assignment to seek new persons to fill vacated positions. The overall goal is fairly simple. The committee needs to hire some new employees. Let's dive into the details. Five members form the search committee. Two persons want to replace a person in the same position that was vacated. Two others want to tweak the position before the search begins. The fifth person wants to find the person then tweak the position. They all want the coach to help them move forward. What's a coach to do?

The scenario is not unusual. When you get five people in a room, you often have differing opinions, beliefs, values, and attitudes—not to mention that the skill levels or interests of the persons involved will likely differ as well. If the group is open to exploration and willing to work toward consensus, a coach can help them focus and move forward. Consider this coaching model as a tool in this scenario:

Building BRIDGES

Building bridges is important when a group comes from different situations and is working to find unity of purpose and a common direction toward harmony, because if you are not building bridges you are likely building barriers. (Note: While we used the BARRIERS model in chapter 5 with individuals and BRIDGES here in chapter 6 for institutions, these tools can be used in either coaching situation.)

Coach To Build
BRIDGES
 Belief Systems
 Relationships
 Intention
 Discover
 Gifts
 Engagement
 Summarize

> Belief Systems
> Relationships
> Intention
> Discover
> Gifts
> Engagement
> Summarize

B—Belief Systems

Gaining clarity about what is really going on and what brings each committee member to his or her position is critically important. It's also important to discern the emotional landscape of those in the decision-making group. Beliefs often limit our perspective and impact our behavior, building barriers instead of bridges. Consider following this coach approach:

Beliefs often limit our perspective and impact our behavior, building barriers instead of bridges.

- Tell me more about your position regarding this assignment.
- What are your concerns about the issue at hand?
- What are your concerns about the position of others regarding this staffing issue?
- What do you need to know about their position?
- What is needed now?

R—Relationships

Coaches work to create a spirit of cooperation and discover what types of relationships already exist with those in the room.

This often provides direction and clarity and helps the coach and each person understand the dynamics at work. (In other words, who are the friends, foes, and family members?) So, taking time to understand and build relationships, observing the group carefully, looking and listening for disconnects between what they say and how they behave will be helpful. Consider a coach approach such as the following:

Coaches work to create a spirit of cooperation and discover what types of relationships already exist among those in the room.

- What do you need the committee to know about you?
- What brings you to serve in this capacity now?
- Who are your heroes in life?
- What relational skills are important for leaders?

I—Intention

Discovering the intention of a group or individual is also important in a coaching scenario. A coach needs to discern the coachability of the group and of the individuals in the group. If the intention of one or more is to sidetrack the group, bring a personal agenda to the group, or sabotage the mission of the group, these intentions need to be surfaced, acknowledged, and dealt with appropriately. Consider this coach approach:

If the intention of one or more is to side-track the group, bring a personal agenda to the group, or sabotage the mission of the group, that needs to be surfaced, acknowledged, and dealt with appropriately.

- What would be the ideal situation here?
- What would be the best version of this job description/ position?
- What would you like to change in the process?
- What would you like to change with this job description?
- What is driving your idea?
- What do we need to resolve today?

D—Discover

Sometimes a group simply needs to explore options together to move forward. Limiting visions/ideas or beliefs often prevent persons or groups from seeing outside, much less beyond the box. It can be a powerful dialogue to discuss what the group knows and then have them discuss what they don't know. Consider this coach approach:

- What are the possibilities here?
- Who are other persons we might talk with about these options?

- How can we discover the benefits/challenges of each option?
- What are the likely consequences if we do not look at other possibilities?
- Which of these options do you value most? (Prioritize the list individually and then as a group and compare results for a consensus direction.)
- How much time/energy are we ready to give to each of the top three options?

What are the possibilities here?

G—Gifts

Discovering the type of gifts/skills needed by a potential leader is critical. What gifts/skills are needed is a place for building consensus and finding a focus. Allowing people to use their true gifts and skills will unleash the true passion for the individuals and group to excel. Consider this coach approach:

- What strengths are we looking for?
- What if we do not find the best skill set for this position?
- Which of these strengths are most important for this position?
- What might be the outcome if we do our assignment well?
- What if we miss the mark?
- How does our decision affect the organization's welfare?

E—Engagement

Coaching is about moving people to action, not just dialogue. Prior to this piece of coaching, the coach needs to have worked hard to make certain every member of the committee has been heard and had the opportunity to respond to each other's responses to the previous explorations.

Consider this coach approach to move them to engagement:

Coaching is about moving people to action, not just dialogue.

- What are we ready to act on now?
- What is needed to make this a successful step now?
- Who will do what by when?
- What is still unresolved?
- What barriers still exist here?
- What do we need to do prior to the next meeting that can move us forward?

This movement forward may be incremental, or it may be radical for the group's progress, but either is great. Working to find commonality among beliefs, limitations, and next steps is the goal here.

S—Summarize

Summary by the person/group being coached is critical to moving forward. Allowing the client to do the summary builds ownership and accountability. The coach needs to listen carefully as each summarizes. If a major disconnect becomes evident or evidence of sabotage lingers, the coach might need to ask permission to offer a challenge to the group that will help them move forward. It might be a homework assignment for reading, self-reflection, or interviewing others. The group, of course, can accept, amend, or deny the challenge. Consider this coach approach:

> * Who can bottom line (i.e., succinctly summarize) discoveries made in this meeting?
> * What are the top three things we decided?
> * Which discovery made the most impact for you?
> * What are our next steps?
> * What do you need now? (Ask each person, and the group as a whole.)

Using the Seven Keys in Coaching

Key 1: What are the needed shifts?

After examining the Ripple model, the coach will listen carefully to see where the group or individuals in the group might be entering this model. Various people or teams in the organization may enter at different places. The coach and those being coached discern where they are and where they want to focus first. To know the needed shifts in a given situation, the group must have a clear outlook on the goals they wish to accomplish. These goals do not have to be written in stone. They can definitely be altered and adjusted, but a good sense of where they want to go needs to be articulated and agreed upon. This is actually the easy part! The hard part: once they have some idea of where they want to go, you and the group must then decide how to get there, and when.

Organizations typically find themselves either trying to move from a maintenance posture of day-to-day activity to a more progressive mission, or moving from desperation of circumstances of finances or shrinking customer base to hope of a more profitable future. The coach's role is to create some waves of hope amidst

Summary by the person/group being coached is critical to moving forward.

Key 1
What are the shifts needed? Now?

the realities of the organization. Such issues open the door for coaching—and particularly with key question 2.

Key 2: What are the shifts about anyway?

Taking the same scenario, let's explore the coach approach when working with this committee around the shifts they have previously identified utilizing key question 1. What factors should a coach be tuned into as the committee or team seek to assess what the shifts are about? Coaches need to keep in their mind the HARMONY framework (see appendices) as a way of making shifts without making waves.

Key 2
What are the shifts about anyway?

Let's clarify the difference here between a team, committee approach, and community approach. What are the distinctives of each type of group as they interact with transformational change?

COMMITTEE APPROACH	TEAM APPROACH	COMMUNITY APPROACH
Focus on preserving the institution	Focus on collaboration and consensus in decision making	Focus on establishing community, belonging
Long-term commitment called for	Short-term commitment	Willing to show up when needed to accomplish community goals
Constitutionally driven (driven by governing documents more than current vision)	Relationship driven	Community driven
Institutional concerns and orientation	Need and task oriented	Fellowship/Community need orientation

Clarity of the issues—the soulful leader checks this out with the committee, team, or community, but also with each individual as they begin this next step of the change process. Consider the following:

- Personal agendas versus group agenda
- Time line
- Sense of urgency
- What is your mission statement?
- What value is added?
- Passion around the issues—both passion of individual committee members and passion of the group
- Potential for sabotage or derailing the conversation

Think again about the scenario raised earlier. The personnel search committee calls for coaching as they begin their assignment to seek new persons to fill vacated positions. The overall goal is fairly simple. This committee needs to hire some new employees. Remember the details. The search committee has five members.

Two persons want to replace a person in the same position that was vacated. Two others want to tweak the position before the search begins. (We have now learned that one of these last two persons wants a walk-around type manager. The other wants the position to be filled by someone who can raise money, do promotion, and be a keynote speaker at community events.) The fifth person wants to find the person, then tweak the position. (This committee member seems to already have a person in mind that he knows and would like to tweak the position just for that person.) The committee wants the coach to help them move forward. What's a coach to do?

Knowing the new information that has surfaced from the committee in previous coaching sessions leads to the conclusion that to move this committee forward requires the following coaching skills:

A. Working toward consensus

- What is resonating with you now?
- What are the top three issues we have discovered that need our attention today?
- How would you prioritize these issues in terms of importance of accomplishing your goals?
- How should we proceed now?
- What are the main tasks and duties of the open positions? Do you want these to change?
- We have surfaced things such as some want one style of leadership and others want another style of leadership. How do we resolve this?
- In the drilling down process (i.e., the coach drills to get clarity, focus, and consensus from each person and group), tension emerges, but resolution and clarity will bring great relief and direction.

B. Clarifying issues and actions

The group identified as their top three issues:

1. Needed time line for employment;
2. Differing thoughts about job description; and
3. Determining what success will look like in this situation.

- What are the disconnects you see here?
- How can we determine what's best for us now?
- What are the basic criteria for this position that are non-negotiable?

- What are the negotiables?
- How's your energy around this now?

C. Keeping the committee focused

(This is a greater challenge with a group than with individuals and demands intense and skilled coaching.) The coach will insistently ask:

- How are we doing?
- What progress are we making here?
- What next steps are emerging?
- What action can we take now?

Key 3: Who needs to know about the shifts?

Supporters and champions of the shifts *and* those who are skeptical about the change need to know. Getting all the needed leadership persons on board with the decisions is critical. It's not essential to have *everyone* embrace the change before you make the needed shifts. In fact, this is a key barrier many groups face—they want to get everyone in the organization on board before they do anything. That will likely never happen, but research tells us that the tipping point for making change in an institutional culture takes about 20 to 25 percent of active membership. Then their families and friends or colleagues and employees will follow those who are trusted and legitimize the new direction. You pick up another 20 to 30 percent of the people here, and the shift can be made. This points out the value of inviting some dissenters or skeptics into the group leading the change process. (See the books *Diffusion of Innovations* and *The Tipping Point*[6] for additional information on this research.) When the skeptics get their concerns addressed and become advocates, their shift generates shifts in others who trust their opinions and leadership.

To accomplish this difficult step, coaching questions might include:

- Who else shares your concerns?
- How can we hear their concerns?
- What do they need to know that we can now provide?
- Who is the best person(s) to share this information or conduct this interview?

Key 3
Who needs to know about the shifts?

Key 4: *What about the dissenters/skeptics?*

Key 4
What do the
dissenters/skeptics
need to know?

This is a crucial question for the leadership team to answer in order to determine and strategize how and when best to respond. Very often those skeptics raise questions or issues that are valuable insights for the leadership team. Often even the leadership team can have a blind spot when it comes to change, or the members of the team may be driven more by their personal agendas than by what is best for the organization. Some coaching questions to get at this include:

- Who are the skeptics?
- What are their top three concerns?
- If we can only address two of the three concerns, which are most important to them?
- What is driving their need to know?
- What does their concern say that we (leadership team) need to hear now?

An example of this came for me (Eddie) when "Mr. B," a declared dissenter to policy and procedural changes in our church, had an epiphany that shifted his opinion. His influence and impact help shift things so the congregation I was serving could move forward. One man and his wife gained a clearer understanding of the situation as a result of hours of conversation, reflection, and prayer. This insight was announced, and the changes and transitions needed to move the organization forward began as ripples in a lake. Mr. and Mrs. B understood and voiced their support. Their family came on board; then their friends and their family's friends turned positive, and the shifts happened!

Key 5
What timing is needed
in making these
shifts?

Key 5: *What timing is needed?*

Timing is significant when introducing and managing change. Discerning the best time to have certain dialogues with certain persons can make or break the power of the moment. Determining coachability is one thing, but determining the right time for this conversation is another thing.

- What are the indicators of the right time?
- Who needs to know?
- When do they need to know?
- How much does each person need to know?

Key 6: Who can help move us forward now?

Change needs cheerleaders, champions, dissenters, and advocates. Influence of others makes a significant impact when introducing and managing change. Coaching questions might include:

Key 6
Who can help us move forward now?

- Who are the influential persons in the group or organization you are seeking to impact with change?
- Who are the legitimizers in the organization?
- Who can help open new doors of opportunity?
- Who are the persons who can make the most impact on the most persons now?
- What support do they need now?

Key 7: What is next?

Coaching seeks to move organizations and leaders forward. Determining *what* is appropriate and *when* is critical in forward movement. Inviting the leadership team and others who have joined the change process to help determine what is next for the organization builds ownership, establishes deepening trust, and creates an atmosphere of hope, anticipation, and possibilities.

Coaching questions might include:

Key 7
What is next?

- What needs to be done first?
- What will make the most impact now?
- What are the benefits of this shift for the organization?
- What are the possibilities now for our organization?
- What do you need from the organization now?
- What does the organization need from you now?
- What are you willing to do now to improve the organization's effectiveness and value?

These seven keys are a standard toolkit for a soulful leader who uses coaching to introduce and manage change. These key questions unlock key issues, values, timelines, and a focus that insures forward movement even amidst diversity. These seven key questions are applicable when working with individuals, families, businesses, and profit and nonprofit organizations. A successful coaching experience hinges on three key factors:

1. Coachability of the person or organization in question
2. Determination of everyone involved to move forward
3. Willingness to face the unfamiliar and walk into the new (as decided by the group)

Making shifts without making waves is a prevalent challenge for families, businesses, individuals, and organizations of all sizes, a challenge found in almost all contexts. This reality hinges on the rapid pace of change being generated in our increasingly pluralistic culture, which is driven in large part by the fast pace and exponential changes brought about by technology. Natalie Gillam puts it this way: "In a world where power is in information and innovation, it is vital that leaders encourage innovation and new ideas and that they value diverse thinking within their team. Without this an organization risks being left behind."[7]

Gillam continues by declaring, "Providing enough opportunities for listening and challenging the status quo is vital, as without these forums it is difficult for people not to become consumed in day-to-day activities and tasks, never engaging with the debate."[8]

Return on Investment for Individuals and Organizations

In these challenging days every business is seeking to get the best return on investments. "According to a recent Sales Performance International survey of sales managers at 134 different companies, inaccurate forecasting had become a big problem for them. In the survey, sales managers cited poor forecasting more often (54 percent) than either declining revenue (49 percent) or inadequate coaching (34 percent)."

Achieving maximum return on investment seems to correlate with following criteria offered by Keith Eades:

Most sales managers strive to meet three success criteria:

1. Make the revenue numbers
2. Forecast sales revenue accurately
3. Coach and develop the right team of people to get the job done.[9]

Too many companies and too many sales managers hire experienced salespeople, believing they know how to sell. However, even the very best salespeople need ongoing coaching, mentoring, and training to maintain their peak performance.[10]

Craig Dowden has determined:

The most effective coaching relationships are client-driven, because what works for the coach may not work for the client (e.g., coachee) in his or her situation. Thus the role of the coach is to ask the right questions to get the coachee to think differently about certain challenges they are facing rather than "telling them what to do" or producing an off-the-shelf solution. Considerable

To know the needed shifts in a given situation, the group must have a clear outlook on the goals they wish to accomplish.

Organizations typically find themselves either trying to move from a maintenance posture to a more progressive mission or moving from desperation to hope of a more successful future.

research and experience has shown that engaging clients as part of the solution maximizes the possibility of their long-term success.[11]

Dowden also discusses four ways coaching is valuable to an organization:

a. Opportunity to engage in fire prevention versus fire fighting
b. Opportunity to brainstorm
c. Opportunity for honest feedback
d. What got you here won't get you there

a. Opportunity to engage in fire prevention versus fire fighting—Dowden finds modern managers are under tremendous pressure and "rarely get the opportunity to engage in an important aspect of their role, which is to think strategically." Many have noted that working with a coach "requires them to set time aside every week, or month, to discuss and think about the 'bigger issues' that are affecting their job."

b. Opportunity to brainstorm—Managers often feel isolated, Dowden explains. A coach can serve as a "trusted advisor" who helps sort through issues and acts as a "sounding board." This "is enormously valuable to the executive, both in terms of raising their self-awareness as well as finding the answers they need by 'talking through' their challenges."

c. Opportunity for honest feedback—Dowden points out that as individuals ascend the corporate ladder, they often receive less open and honest feedback. "Bringing in an external coach allows a mechanism for gathering this information to occur, such as via 360–degree feedback or psychometric/personality assessment," he concludes.

d. What got you here won't get you there—Top performing employees often "struggle mightily when they are thrust into a management role," Dowden reports. Coaching plays a crucial role in helping develop leadership and people management skills, through increasing managers' own self-awareness and helping them recognize that their views of the world may not be shared by others. "Thus, coaching supports the manager in leveraging the strengths of the organizational talent pool by engaging with each individual team member in a way that matches his or her needs," he says.

Dowden advises that once an organization has decided to use a coach, it should determine its goals for the process, decide who is going to receive the coaching, and find well-credentialed coaches. Several crucial questions and issues need to be addressed to maximize the opportunity for a successful coaching relationship. A partial list of things to consider would include:

The coach's role is to create some waves of hope amidst the realities of the organization.

Working toward consensus

Getting all the needed leadership persons on board with the decisions is critical.

When the skeptics get their concerns addressed and become advocates, their shift generates shifts in others who trust their opinion and leadership.

Very often those skeptics raise questions or issues that are valuable insights for the leadership team. Often even the leadership team can have a blind spot when it comes to change, or the members of the team may be driven more by their personal agendas than by what is best for the organization.

Timing is significant when introducing and managing change.

a. Clarity of purpose
b. Who receives the coaching?
c. Credentials

a. Clarity of purpose—Essentially, what is the goal of the coaching assignment for your organization? Often, many organizations (and coaches) get involved without truly understanding the expectations of the other party. It is essential, or at least highly recommended, to work out an "Accountability Contract" that outlines the roles that each party (e.g., coach, client, and corporate client) will play in this engagement. Recent research in 2008 by the American Management Association (AMA), www.amanet.org, showed that the clearer the reason a company had for embarking on a coaching program, the better the programmatic results.

b. Who receives the coaching?—A survey conducted by the AMA concluded that the three most common groups to receive coaching are high potential employees, problem performers, and executives. However, as with any leadership development activity, it is important to consider the message being sent to the rest of the organization if coaching is only being provided to one of these groups. For example, if coaching is only given to the top performers, this may be quite demotivating for the rest of the company. Conversely, if it is only used to address "problem employees," it may be viewed quite negatively and may even carry a stigma that will be difficult to discard at a later date. Thus, the potential implications of utilizing this type of development activity on the corporate culture should be considered in detail before moving forward.

c. Credentials—The field of coaching currently does not have any universally accepted qualifications or credentialing process. Although this may sound troublesome, interestingly, research suggests that qualifications are the lowest rated item of concern for organizations when selecting an external coach (with previous and similar coaching experience rated number one.[12]) However, when faced with an endless selection of seemingly strong candidates, what are the most important differentiators? To answer this question, let's consider the American Management Association's global study on coaching (http://www.amanet. org). In their review, they picked ten common "selection criteria" for coaches and examined whether the coaches meeting the criteria had significantly greater impact on future market performance of the organizations they were coaching. Some of the criteria that they looked at included coaching certifications, accreditation, recommendations from a trusted source, university degrees in a related field, etc. Of these, only three had a significant statistical relationship with market performance:

1. Business experience,
2. Consulting experience, and
3. Having a Ph.D.

Although the first two have been widely viewed as being important in the past, the last criteron may seem somewhat surprising. However, as mentioned by the study authors, "one possible reason for this is that Ph.D.s bring a level of expertise to a field that has very low barriers to entry"[13] Based on the above, it appears that these three factors are the most important when it comes to maximizing the ROI (return on investment) of coaching in terms of the bottom line.

Dowden concludes that coaching can tremendously benefit an organization: "Developing people is the most important thing an organization can do and finding effective and empowering ways to positively impact individual and team performance is an essential component of true success."[14]

Don't forget to look in the back of the book for a resource list of coaching, consulting, and training companies that may fit your needs.

Who are the legitimizers in the organization?

Determining what is appropriate and when it is appropriate are critical in forward movement.

SECTION
THREE

Sustaining
Soulful Leadership

Sustaining Soulful Leadership

Change and transition have a way of overwhelming leaders and organizations, not to mention achieving transformation. The daily demands of work very often distract leaders and organizations from intentionally discerning and charting the future. While their needs for change might be clear, their honorable daily work must be done. This often leaves little time or energy for creating a future filled with hope rather than despair or anxiety. Creating sacred space and a priority to slow down and work on change is essential. This is the power of a coaching relationship.

This final chapter is dedicated to principles based on the coach approach to introducing and managing change. Over the last decade many major corporations and businesses have been seeking to activate the soul in the workplace. This is evidenced by the vast array of books on the subject and the numerous websites addressing the connection between faith and work. (See appendices.) Sustaining soulful leadership is achieved by preserving and following these principles as work agendas and priorities for resources are decided. This will help sustain and continue to move you forward with intentionality and a future focus.

> The power of a coaching relationship is creating sacred space, and a priority to slow down and to work on change is essential.

Reviewing the Traits of a Soulful Leader

As a review, here are the foundational traits of a soulful leader:

- Soulful leaders respond rather than react to the need for change. That is, they do not have knee-jerk reactions but

Soulful leaders

- respond rather than react to the need for change
- lead more by asking powerful, discerned questions
- lead more by example than by e-mail
- preserve confidentiality and integrity
- encourage and allow storytelling
- are always learning
- are accountable
- set goals and objectives
- connect body, mind, and soul
- are transforming

rather thoughtful and intentional responses when the winds of change blow around them.

- Soulful leaders lead more by asking powerful, discerned questions than by handing out demands or telling others what to do.
- Soulful leaders lead more by example than by e-mail.
- Soulful leaders preserve confidentiality and integrity. They coach by working from the agenda of the person or organization being coached.
- Soulful leaders encourage and allow storytelling as a way of building community that ultimately co-creates their future or that of the organization.
- Soulful leaders are always learning, having the attitude, "I am a student and steward of life!" They invest in training, coaching, and consulting to be on top of new trends and effective leadership strategies.
- Soulful leaders are accountable.
- Soulful leaders set goals and objectives that are communicated to the entire organization.
- Soulful leaders connect body, mind, and soul.
- Soulful leaders flex their spiritual muscles, physical muscles, and psychological muscles.
- Soulful leaders are transforming.

Brian McLaren, a pastor, author and twenty-first–century thought leader, captured the essence and impact of the cultural shifts all around us when he penned the following words on his blog at www.deepshift.com.

We Are in Deep Shift

A time of transition
Rethinking
re-imagining
and re-envisioning
A time for asking new questions
and seeking answers
that are both new and old
fresh and seasoned
surprising and familiar

What does it mean, in today's world, to be a follower of God in the way of Jesus? What does it mean to be a faith community engaged in the holistic, integral mission of God in our world today?

How do we, as individuals and organizations, respond faithfully to the crises facing our world?

What is our duty to God, ourselves, our families, our neighbors, our enemies, and our planet in light of Jesus' radical message of the kingdom of God?

How can we engage in personal formation and theological reformulation for global transformation?

Living in deep shift can be exhilarating and energizing, but it can also be disorienting and frightening.[1]

Capturing Your Stories—Making Your Shifts Happen

May I (Eddie) be personal with you for a moment? May I share something of my story with you that describe shifts I'm facing?

As of this writing, my family has more who have passed from this earth than those of us left on this earth. Many of us left are faced with aging bodies, declining health, and moving into retirement years. While this reality brings some grief and loss, it also brings new opportunities and opens new doors as a new season of life unfolds. I look forward to an early retirement from denominational and local church service and partnering with colleagues to launch another dimension of a consulting and coaching career.

I've tracked cultural shifts professionally for several decades and have applied them to faith communities and have helped many communities make needed shifts to improve their effectiveness and efficiency in light of cultural shifts. During these decades of service I have found a void for similar services in the business and nonprofit organizations. The remaining years of my career will be focused on coach training and coaching services to help leaders and organizations make needed shifts that will ensure effectiveness and fulfillment in accomplishing their mission.

These personal shifts really evolve from those of my family who have passed. They were leaders of passion, committed to making a difference in their occupations or careers. Their departures were felt by the organizations they served, and few, if any, stepped into the gaps their deaths created. I want to help fill the gaps and restore countless thousands of workers across the country who are not experiencing fulfillment personally, spiritually, or vocationally in their careers. They want to make an impact, but they are only logging hours and waiting for the workday to pass. Restoring others by deepening their souls so they can make deep shifts that will impact others is my future.

I want to watch business owners and managers wake up with excitement about going to work because they know they will impact others that day! I want to coach leaders who are seeking to break unhealthy or unproductive cycles in life and help them discover what's next and what will light their fires and fuel their

> What then are your stories? What are the deep shifts you are faced with today?

hearts with hope and fulfillment! I want to watch businesses discover ways not only to impact the souls of those they employ, but to nurture their dreams and hopes in ways the businesses/organizations significantly impact the souls of the institutions and the communities in which they serve. What does that look like? I'm not sure…but I know we can explore together and celebrate those connections we make that empower others!

What then are your stories? What are the deep shifts you are faced with today?

React or proactively respond?

- At home?
- In your family?
- At work?
- At play?
- In your community?
- In your finances?
- In your community of faith?
- In other areas of your life?

Ask rather than tell.

React or Proactively Respond

Soulful leaders take a more proactive response to the waves of change.

When the waves of change begin to roll through a town, organization, business, or church, the employees and often the leaders get into a reactive posture. Reaction is often based on emotions or the immediate needs of the moment and is primarily characterized by a knee-jerk reaction without considering the big picture or doing much reflection on the situation. Soulful leaders take a more proactive response to the waves of change. They resist a knee-jerk reaction and take time to reflect, inquire of others concerning their perspectives, and explore the benefits and consequences of the changes that are emerging. Response is based on the core values of the organization, the purposes of the business, and the hopes and realities of the future.

The soulful leader reflects more and asks more questions of the constituents rather than making declarations.

Exhibiting patience, discernment, and perseverance makes a difference in tense situations. Reactionary and self-deceptive leadership generates even more anxiety. This unhealthy leadership creates more emotional situations because the group involved or the core values of the organization are ignored or overlooked.

Often the reactionary leader ends up spouting forth demands, requirements, and more work out of fear without consideration of the impact on others. The soulful leader reflects more and asks more questions of the constituents rather than making declarations. He or she is intentional about making decisions and allocating resources that move the organization forward, and seeks the best for all involved whenever possible.

Ask Rather than Tell

A significant distinctive of soulful leadership is the use of the coach approach in the midst of change. The soulful leader is motivated by a mental and emotional value shift that impacts his or her leadership strategies. The soulful leader believes and trusts that those involved, if healthy and open to coaching, are likely to have some of the answers to the challenges facing the organization in light of likely changes. The soulful leader believes that inviting others to explore options and discover benefits and consequences themselves creates a collaborative atmosphere. Peers have a voice and feel empowered. The organization can then benefit from the creative and collective wisdom of those in the organization. Such, more often than not, creates an atmosphere that builds ownership of shifts that might need to happen to effectively deal with the change on the horizon. This atmosphere is a vital ingredient of making only small ripples instead of uncontrollable waves when change presents itself to an individual or an organization.

The realities of this shift in the way leadership is exhibited create feelings of trust, gratitude, integrity, and empowerment. This is because the soulful leader has been willing to listen to persons involved and invited them to join in brainstorming possible solutions to the challenges being faced. More often than not, a leader's value to an organization increases when soulful leadership principles are followed. That leader's integrity is enhanced rather than diminished. Working from a foundation of peer-learning, collaboration, and integrity energizes the leader and organization to leap forward in function and effectiveness.

Working from and for Integrity

Integrity among leadership is a rare virtue in today's world. North America has encountered the horrors of multiple Enron-type scandals. Political, educational, and ecclesiastical scandals abound. As we write this in early 2009, the news is filled with scandals in Washington, D.C.; Chicago; and South Carolina. The former governor of Illinois was accused of "selling the Senate seat" vacated by our new president. Corporate executives are mismanaging "bail out" monies and providing millions of dollars in bonuses while many Americans are losing their homes due to faulty mortgage plans offered by these same executives. The South Carolina governor revealed a trip to Argentina to see his mistress, much to the distress of his family and his political party.

Soulful leaders who work from the coach approach manifest and value the virtues of a soulful leader earn and live by integrity. Now, no one is perfect. Mistakes are often made in the heat of rapid change, but soulful leaders often have persons in their circle of friends and colleagues who challenge them with accountability to maintain integrity, to stop and reflect before reacting, and to

> A leader's value to an organization increases when soulful leadership principles are followed.

> A leader's integrity is enhanced rather than diminished when soulful leadership principles are followed.

> Integrity among leadership is a rare virtue in today's world.

ask powerful questions rather than just making quick decisions and handing out commands.

Soulful leaders value human creativity and insights. They believe that human beings confronted by change can become bitter and resentful of the change or they can become better and resolve to embrace change in ways that improve life. The shifts being created by change generate powerful stories of change and transition by each person impacted by the changes. Soulful leaders understand that creating forums for these new stories to be shared creates a community of trust, companionship, and redemption that restores and celebrates the new and knows how to connect the past to the present and future. Saying good-bye to the old is as important as saying hello to the new. *A soulful leader works with those involved to experience the power of storytelling.*

The Power of Storytelling

Annette Simmons offers organizations many resources and forums for crafting and experiencing the power of storytelling.[2] *Soulful leaders know the power of story.* Story is a way of saying good-bye and saying hello. Powerful coaching questions can help facilitate peer learning and sharing around significant learnings, discoveries, benefits, and consequences encountered by change. Storytelling is the number one means of communicating anything. According to the International Storytelling Center, you need to learn how to tell six stories:

- who I am stories
- why I am here stories
- my vision story
- teaching stories
- values in action stories
- "I know what you are thinking" stories[3]

Some of the powerful coaching questions to elicit and formulate stories might include:

- What are the shifts bringing to you?
- What are the shifts taking from you?
- What causes you to engage at a deeper level?
- What are the benefits of the shifts for you? Others?
- How can we honor our past in the present and future we are creating?
- What is the best version of the new we are creating that you can see now?
- What can you take with you into the new?
- What will you share with your children/grandchildren about this new thing?

Margin notes:
Soulful leaders value human creativity and insights.

What can you take with you into the new?

A soulful leader works with those involved to experience the power of storytelling.

- Who are those you want to tell about the new being created?
- What will you tell them?
- What keeps coming to you that you choose to ignore?
- What are the choices you make that keep you stuck?
- How can we make this happen?
- What are the likely benefits?

Sharing our human stories and even seeking where our human stories connect with divine stories creates a powerful community. The community becomes the seedbed for birthing the new, for celebrating the collaborative creation, and for growing stronger through the challenge of change.

The Power of Community

Transformation happens in and through community. A community can shape the future by their voice. They can help actually make the changes needed and deepen their ownership as their voice and hopes are addressed. Now certainly we need to be realistic here—not everyone's preferences are possible, but they are certainly more likely to be heard, if not included, through the powerful voice of the community. Community is power. Gaining momentum to let go of the past and move toward the future is enhanced and generated through community. People sharing their hurts and hopes, generated by the waves of change, is essential to create forums for new personal, professional, organizational, and spiritual growth.

Again, coaching questions can help unleash the power of the community. However, soulful leaders and coaches may offer words of encouragement, hope, and affirmation as their peers choose to engage in building the new rather than being enraged over the changes being presented.

Soulful leaders understand that during change people need to be heard, but also need to be encouraged and affirmed. Celebrating their contributions, insights, and willingness to move forward means a lot to persons who are losing something in order to gain or contribute to the new. I (Eddie) recently talked with one of my coaching clients who works on staff in a church. The church greatly needed to make some classroom changes to position themselves for stronger numerical growth in their inner city location. We had been coaching around this for several sessions. One day she called to celebrate a powerful move one of their older charter members had made publicly. The elderly lady had a powerful insight as her class discussed the need for them to move so another group could use their room. The charter member stood and voted first in the church business meeting where this decision to move forward and move classes was to be made. She

Transformation happens in and through community.

Soulful leaders understand that during change people need to be heard, but also need to be encouraged and affirmed.

Community is a powerful teacher, and the human and organizational stories need to be shared and celebrated.

voted in favor of the move. Her influence was powerful. The class members followed her lead. The minister I was coaching decided this was a vital piece of their church history and wrote a formal letter affirming the decision made by this lady and her class. The letter, signed by all clergy and committee members, was presented to the women in a worship setting and attached to their church history records. What a time of celebration, affirmation, encouragement, and empowerment! Community is a powerful teacher, and the human and organizational stories need to be shared and celebrated.

Pressing Forward Rather Than Untangling the Past

The power of soulful leaders is manifested through their leadership skills, their sensitivity, their value of the opinions and contributions of others, and their efforts to be more responsive than reactionary. Another valuable characteristic of soulful leaders is *the intention of moving people and organizations forward in keeping with their organizational core values* and *not being consumed by untangling the past or debating the change.* So often change is forced externally by new cultural, economic, demographic, or political realities. The leaders of so many individuals, organizations, and churches really do not want to bring hurt upon their employees or membership, so they back away from change. They remain compliant by staying in their own and their organization's comfort zones. *A soulful leader wants to move forward while listening,* being sensitive to and engaging the voice of peers in decision-making. In reality, the time often comes when the leader has to make a tough decision. The collaborative efforts prove insufficient for an array of reasons. The leader has to make what is often a painful and unpopular decision.

A checklist and self-evaluation tool is appropriate here. Where are you in your shifts—your journey toward being a soulful leader—at work, at home, in recreation, at church, in your community? Use an X to rank on the continuums below where you are now. Use a Y to indicate where you want to be in a year. The premise of the book is that making shifts without making waves involves shifts in you as leader. *Internal* shifts allow *external* shifts around you. Internal shifts opens the doorway for external shifts to occur.

> A soulful leader has the intention of moving people and organizations forward in keeping with their organizational core values rather than being consumed by untangling the past or debating the change.

> A soulful leader brings transformation to those they invest in and intentionally touch.

Talking _____	Listening
Telling _____	Asking
Dictating _____	Discovering
Assigning _____	Inviting
Change _____	Change and Transition
Change and Transition _____	Transformation
Building Barriers _____	Building Bridges
Reactive _____	Proactive
Alignment _____	Attunement

Soulful leaders bring transformation to those they invest in and intentionally touch. Soulful leaders can make a significant difference and can make shifts without making overwhelming waves if they follow principles in this book. Again, some situations—but far from all—call for radical and immediate shifts due to economic or other issues related to the unhealthy patterns and people in the organization. Such a person or organization is not usually coachable or responsive to soulful leadership, and the leaders have to move forward regardless of the opinion of the group. If, however, the group stays open to collaboration, exhibits the skills of good and healthy decision-making, and moves forward rather than simply fighting or choosing not to let go of the past, then birthing the new is highly likely and can be done without the impact of overwhelming waves.

What are your next steps as a soulful leader?

Overwhelming and exponential change is characteristic of our times and calls for the deep conviction of a committed soulful leader with forward-thinking constituents who desire to build a future for their children and grandchildren. Soulful leaders are committed to life-long learning—facing new challenges with intellectual curiosity, intentional skill sets, and a deep soul. Soulful leaders also covenant with others to maintain a healthy work-life balance so that they take care of themselves, allowing them to invest in and empower others. Deepening souls in leaders empower them to make and influence deep shifts and transformations in others. The impact of one soul on another soul—be it individual, family, organization, or church, brings transformation of heart, head, healing, and hope. What better gift to bring and to be!

The impact and influence of soulful leaders ripples through many and continues to impact for some time. For instance, recall the interviews with the pilot who landed his plane on the Hudson. Family, spouses, children, friends, colleagues, neighbors, etc., brought words of appreciation and gratitude to the pilot. The children still had parents, the parents still had children, the grandparents…and the ripples on impact and influence continue.

Hope is birthed by the leaders and by the visions of those who choose to respond well to meaningful change rather than fight it just to preserve their comfort zones and allow them to rest in the fields of familiarity. Making shifts without making waves is possible when guided by soulful leaders and persons with a deep abiding view of the future. What are your next steps as a soulful leader? Who can help you achieve your dreams and create the new story for your life and organization?

Maybe a fitting conclusion to sustaining soulful leadership includes when to send out the flare for help. We all have limitations on time, energy, or resources when it comes to managing and introducing change. So here's another checklist for you to consider. Send out the cry for help when…

> • You or the organization is stuck
> • You lose the ability to be stretched or to stretch others
> • You lose passion or energy for the new
> • You feel drained
> • You continually have more of an inward focus than an outward focus
> • You experience overwhelming resistance to change
> • You are doing the same thing over and over and expecting change
> • You have limited leadership to make needed impact and cast needed influence
> • You are networking with pioneers who see and cast transformational ideas
> • You feel a need for greater objectivity and an outsider's perspectives

Who can help you achieve your dreams and create the new story for your life and organization?

If you are experiencing any of the situations above, hire a coach and experience the power of coaching that moves you forward. Find someone who can look at your situation without the clouded emotions or turfism typical of persons in a given organization. If you have recognized yourself in three or more of the circumstances in the checklist, certainly the time has come to look for a coach.

EPILOGUE

Soulful Leaders Create Transformation

Transformation, Impact, Influence—Personal Journeys

Soulful leadership is about transformation—not just thinking "outside the box" but living "beyond the box" and therefore positively influencing, impacting, and inspiring those around you to live the same. While completing this manuscript we experienced a super illustration of this type of leadership.

About 3:35 p.m. on Friday, January 16, 2009, Captain Chesley "Sully" Sullenberger on US Airways flight 1549 made a transforming decision in a given moment in time. The engines of the aircraft had died (apparently due to birds being sucked into the engines on take-off from LaGuardia Airport). The plane was already in flight, and the captain and co-pilot were now faced with critical decisions: Where do we land? How do we land? When do we land? And how do we protect the 155 persons onboard the plane?

> Soulful leadership is about transformation—not just thinking "outside the box."

Captain Sully followed the principles of a soulful leader. Drawing from his vast experience, internal discernment, and expert skills, he trusted his heart along with his intellect as he reached out for help. He proved that not only could he think "outside the box," but he was willing to live "beyond the box" by following through on his creative thinking and implementing the counsel of others. Reaching out for help was a key element. The result was what is now being called "Miracle on the Hudson River." The captain and co-pilot landed the plane on the Hudson River in a way that was smooth and almost as efficient as it would have been on the tarmac of the airport. Now, certainly the logical and traditional mode of landing a plane was to land that type of plane on an airport runway. However, in this situation, circumstances suddenly changed and called for another way of landing the plane. There was no time or engine power to take the plane back to the airport.

How did the pilot deal with such a challenging situation? Other pilots and investigators confirm that the pilot of flight 1549 made the right decision at the right time. The result was that everyone survived the crash! The plane without power glided to a fairly calm landing on the Hudson River. Some might call this living into a *"kairos* moment"—where everything lines up for the perfect plan to come together. Soulful leaders live to create and experience such moments even though they might often feel it's "beyond the box."

New challenges call for new leadership styles. For the most part in past decades leaders led more by gathered information (which now changes minute by minute) and by being reactive to the information. This was the leadership model available in those years.

Too frequently leaders seek to please their community or colleagues rather than decide with the community of the world in mind. Often models of leading are driven by fear and issues of control rather than desires to empower others to experience freedom, fulfillment, hope, and health. Soulful Leaders today empower others to follow their dreams, callings, and instincts assures forward movement rather than staying stuck or inward focused.

Captain Sully modeled much of what we mean by soulful leadership when he trusted the crew, trusted the plane, found and trusted the water, and followed his instinct and training, which allowed the plane to land on the water and offered a much greater chance of a safe landing than trying to return to the known and trusted tarmac. Captain Sully trusted what he knew and followed his heart in the face of deep challenges. Learning to live "beyond the box" and one's comfort zone is essential in becoming a soulful leader.

> Soulful leaders live to create and experience such moments even though they might often feel it's "beyond the box."

A Glimpse into the Authors' Transformations

As a final word, Eddie and Randy want to share with our readers somewhat of a coaching demonstration. We will share a glimpse of the transformations we have experienced over more than a decade of learning to walk into our fears, challenge our biases and assumptions, heighten our awareness of personal dysfunctions and unhealthy coping skills, and embracing the new dreams planted in our souls.

Ever since the idea of this book was first birthed, it has been our desire to address the issue of change, transition, and transformation in the church world (represented by Eddie's voice) and in the business world (represented by Randy's voice). We firmly believe the principles shared here are practical and powerful tools for transformation regardless of the world you are a leader in. It is also our observation that all organizations and all leaders are faced with the need and probability of change. We also observe that what is needed is not just more leaders, more management, or more vision. What seems to be the greatest need as we face the seismic shifts we are facing is a group of committed soulful leaders who desire and know how to build new dreams, discover consensus among those touched by change, and move everyone and their organizations forward. The movements forward will certainly be built on the successes of the past, but the effectiveness of the vision for tomorrow will come from deep within. Birthing the future now is filled with steep learning curves for all, calls for sacrifices from all, and requires a desire from all to birth the new. We have listened to our "baby kick" and we want to share with you now some of the transformations we have (and continue to) experience that has invigorated us in ways and taken us to places we never imagined.

As authors of this book, Randy and Eddie want to share something of their transformation over the last decade by addressing some questions.

> Birthing the future now is filled with steep learning curves for all, calls for sacrifices from all, and a desire from all to birth the new.

- What transformations have occurred in the last decade?
- What created these shifts?
- How has the transformation changed your life? Career?
- How have you made the shifts called for?
- What worked?
- What did not work?
- What's next for you now?

"Life happens" and "Life is hard" are two clichés that summarize the attitude of many during these challenging days of global and local economic, social, cultural, and organizational shifts. Many become disillusioned, if not resentful, of the shifts that are so often seemingly "beyond our control" or "beyond our reach or pay grade." Our culture is increasingly birthing times and circumstances that call us to newness and transformation. Soulful leaders create transformation as we create safe places, and, sometimes, ongoing coaching relationships that are intentional in discerning together next steps and what forward movement will look like.

These are often divine appointments and filled with teachable moments that fuel dreams, inspire change, and open our hearts, minds, and souls for needed shifts to occur. Your authors, Eddie and Randy, have experienced this transformation over the last fifteen-plus years as we have challenged each other, created safe places for struggles of the soul, and are now living into dreams. We want to share something of our stories of personal and professional transformation in hopes of inspiring and letting you know we "practice what we teach."

In this coaching demonstration we want to share with you our moves from our pinches to our dreams. You will see us experiencing a retooling and refreshment of head, heart, and soul. We will share how discovering inspiration and hope has characterized some of the shifts. We hope this helps you visualize what a coaching relationship might look like—at least a short vignette from our coaching conversations. Watch our www. soulful-leadership.com Web site for updates and podcasts of teaching/coaching tips.

> The power of choice and the collaboration with others allow us to do greater things together than if we simply stand alone.

Coaching Conversation—Moving from Pain to Purpose

Eddie (coach): Randy, how would you describe your transformation over the last fifteen years? What worked and what didn't work?

Randy (person being coached): My journey has been long, difficult, and painful at times. I have had to learn how to integrate head and heart and push ego out of the way. Many of my coping skills and attitudes needed to be reframed and realigned. At times anger and resentment would motivate me to get things done, but I never felt satisfied or complete. I believe we were using the Ripple model before we had even thought about these methodologies. I was the *king of denial!* I had *multiple barriers* and *false beliefs* that kept me stuck in a vicious cycle. I finally got sick of the pain and my *awareness slowly began to improve.* Turning my resentment into gratitude has taken me years as I continue to follow what motivates me and fuels my passion. At times this was walking away from a big paycheck and doing other things that allowed me to search internally and begin to see and feel where I was being called. I have learned that I must do things that excite me and involve personal relationships, servitude, and constant learning. Without a big learning curve, I have found that I get bored and lose my focus and energy.

I have learned that I needed to *give myself permission to try new things* and experiment. I worked in hi-tech; taught Pilates; served as a mental health associate in a lock-down acute psychiatric hospital; took time to paint with acrylics, write, and work on my coaching and training certifications. This was more about *my own discoveries* and not being peer-pressured into what I thought I should be doing or accomplishing. There were extreme days of profound loss and despair as

I continued to *listen to my heart and redefine my beliefs* into a more authentic way of living. For years, I would say I was only surviving and doing very little living.

Eddie (coach): What in coaching worked for you?

Randy (person being coached): I am an experiential learner. I need to talk things out and allow myself time to embrace my internal and external shifts. This is the power of coaching for me. Coaching allows me to think out loud in a safe environment with an objective listener. The coach approach is the way of the future in my opinion, but is extremely hard work. If a person really wants to change and make some shifts toward authentic transformation, the person must unlearn things he or she may have been doing for a very long time and replace them with new attitudes, behaviors, beliefs, and skill-sets. This is much easier said than done. It has been my experience that this cannot be done alone, thus the value of a coach. My integrity, *accountability, and spiritual hunger increased* as I became more aware and aligned with an authentic belief system and way of looking at life.

Eddie (coach): What are your dreams now?

Randy (person being coached): I never thought about being a coach. Coaching really found me. And I never thought about writing, that is for sure! Living into my dream is about helping others make shifts in their lives to be better and to lead better. I have been blessed to have people in my life help me to see some of the extremely stupid decisions that I have made that at times have held me back or taken me in a direction that really was not where I wanted to go. Fear and shame are powerful feelings that at times caused me to be impulsive and reactionary. Such emotional responses always led me to painful pinches. I have learned it is certainly OK to fall down and fail. It is part of the process. It really is a process in which every day I am reminded that I am only as good as my last decision. The power of choice and the collaboration with others allows us to do greater things together than if we simply stand alone. I love coaching, consulting, and training and have plans for more writing projects regarding coaching spiritual travelers. I have created an animated character that I call "the Spiritual Bandit."

I envisioned this character, this Robin Hood type do-gooder that is fun and creative. A mischievous-type creature with an adventurous spirit in the fight against good and evil frames his personality. He is a bandit in the positive sense, not the negative—not a thief or robber, but rather exactly the opposite: winning in the fight against our struggles, our pains, and pitfalls. He is a kindred spirit in "taking down the bad guys"—defeating the false self and allowing the true self to shine. I wanted to create a character that would be appealing to all age groups and could assist in teaching valuable life lessons.

As a coach, we are taught to dream big! One day I would love to see my Bandit friend used as a teaching tool in the form of animation and storyboards.

Eddie (coach): Thanks for sharing this with us. Now can you summarize what are the characteristics of a soulful leader you now embody? What are your next steps?

Randy (person being coached): I am grateful for my shifts that the coaching experience has taught me. It has opened new and exciting doors. I plan to continue to walk with courage and know that it is OK to be vulnerable. It is in those vulnerable "soft" times that we can make the most shifts in attitudes and behavior that empower transformation. When I become bullet-proof and ego begins to get in the way, I have learned to reach out and admit that this is a red flag for me and is robbing me of the opportunity for authentic conversations and collaboration. Being accountable and stepping outside of the cycle of blame have been two of my biggest shifts in embracing my goal to be a soulful leader. To do this I had to embrace surrender and gratitude. The key for me is keeping people in my life that feed and nurture my "True Self." When good things happen, my false self loves to attempt to work its way into my life and sabotage. We all have elements of the saboteur in our lives. If you think you don't, go back to chapter 5 and look at the BARRIERS again. If you think you do not have any barriers, this is a blind spot for you! This is where you must FACE, MAKE, and EMBRACE these issues and work through them. Our addictions, dysfunctions, and blind spots definitely affect our personal and professional lives. It is all about knowing these, labeling these, and getting in spiritual alignment so we can be our very best, walk into our destiny, and be the soulful leaders of tomorrow for revolutionary transformation.

Coaching Conversation—Moving from Telling to Asking

Now we will change roles—for, indeed, we have done so in these later years, as Randy has received his coach certification, too.

Randy (coach): Eddie, how would you describe your transformation over the last fifteen years?

Eddie (person being coached): My shifts have been internal and external as well as personal and professional. Early on in our conversations I felt like I had the answers and I was to "tell you" and get you to agree with me about issues of faith, life, economics, or whatever the issues might be. Much of my professional training had reinforced this mind-set. It was quickly evident to me that this was not working too well in communicating or connecting with you. In fact, the assumption that I had the answers you needed actually sabotaged at times my really being able to hear what you were saying to me. My assumption was that if you would only listen to what I was trying to tell you, then you would succeed in solving the problems we discussed. So often this prevented me from connecting with you and you connecting with me.

Over time, after butting my head against that wall, out of desperation I started "asking" questions and soon discovered that at least we could talk without arguing. This epiphany coincided with an invitation to have a coach and to begin to learn something about coaching. WOW—what a discovery and a relief the experience of being coached had for me. I learned what makes a powerful coaching question and what the benefits of coaching had on me, making shifts that were transforming to me personally, spiritually, and professionally. This shift impacted my home relationships, friendships, and the way I functioned in my job as a consultant.

Randy (coach): How did you get into coaching?

Eddie (person being coached): I must confess first of all that I was a real skeptic of the impact of coaching—being that most coaching is done by phone and I have been such a face-to-face person. But, boy, am I believer now that coaching by phone with a coach I may never meet face to face can be life changing and career changing! The experience of having a coach and bringing my personal agenda to each call offered me focus I've never known. Focus came to my career in ways that empowered, energized, and created a retooling. The coaching focus has now birthed nine books, multiple sources of income, and powerful professional relationships beyond my "day job." Coaching has allowed me to travel across the country to coach business and church leader clients. Coaching has fueled me with dreams that allow me to enter each day (well, most every day) with renewed energy and expectation.

Personally, having a coach (and, by the way, every coach needs a coach) even now has proven to inspire me, motivate me, and create pathways of being proactive rather than reactive to circumstances. For instance, I had to have major surgery two years ago. I faced the threats of death, disability, or an extended recovery that, for many patients in similar circumstances, would likely include depression. I chose to hire a coach to walk with me during these months. I am now doing very well, and—though my recovery lasted over a year—I never got depressed. I never lost my zest for life or my vision for my life and career. In fact, I am certain that those fifteen-to-twenty-minute coaching calls (that was all I had energy for) kept me focused on the future enough to keep me out of depression. What a gift those powerful questions were for me during those challenging and often "dark" days!

Randy (coach): Eddie, how are you living your dream now?

Eddie (person being coached): This book is evidence of living my dream. I have wanted to work with you in ways that would share with a larger audience the discoveries we have helped each other make over the last decades. The overwhelming success of our first writing collaboration, the follow-up seminars and workshops, then the occasional articles and the coaching sessions we do together have given me "new wind in my sails" and have proven to me that our journey—as difficult as it has been some days—is not without meaning and purpose. We now have the opportunity to influence thousands of persons across the country—in fact we just had a planning conversation to be guests on our first blog radio show and will be co-leading a workshop soon with a person who has national recognition and is a frequent guest on the Oprah show. Who would have ever thought it?

I'm also living my dream of influencing more consistently those in the day-to-day grind and challenge of family life and work life. So many of these stressed or stuck workers can benefit from the forward focus of coaching rather than wrestling with the untangling of the past that is the route counseling often pursues with them. I am convinced that these challenging and changing times in which we now live are prime opportunities and fertile fields for coaching to impact lives, restore dreams, and retool businesses and organizations to a more fulfilling experience.

Randy (coach): Thanks for sharing this with us. Now, can you summarize what are the characteristics of a soulful leader you now embody? What are your next steps?

Eddie (person being coached): My next steps are to continue my coaching and coach training and explore new avenues of its power and impact. I also plan to continue my consulting with organizations—profit and nonprofit—as I seek to make a difference in the world and help organizations, families, and leaders make shifts without making too many unnecessary waves. My personal transformation continues as I learn to live by the lessons I have learned through the tough times and celebrations of life and career. The power of coaching continues to invite me to see my divine destiny and to walk into it without fear.

* * * * *

Change has indeed come to America and the world in this decade. Families, companies, churches, and communities are learning to live by and through new challenges and opportunities. What kind of world would we live in if we have transformed leaders and families transforming the institutions and organizations of which they are a part? The choice is ours as soulful leaders. We are called to make the right decisions or make our decisions right. What is your decision?

APPENDICIES

Toolkit for
Soulful Leaders

HARMONY Model and Powerful Coaching Questions

H earing others
- Who needs to be in the conversation?
- What are their assumptions about the challenge?
- What's the best setting that assures them they are being heard?
- How can we best listen to them?

A ssessing the situation to find focus
- What are the pinches here?
- What is really going on?
- What will it take to move forward for each person/group?

R esponding to questions/concerns
- What do you need to know now?
- What are your primary concerns/questions?
- What is needed now?
- Who can help you with your concerns/questions?

M ovement forward through decisions by the group
- What will move us forward in this dialogue now?
- What are the criteria for a good decision?
- How can we help each other now?
- What is needed by each person in the group now?
- Who else can you share your insights with now?

O ptions to explore to build ownership
- What are the possibilities here?
- What options are before us?
- What are the consequences of exploring each option?
- What are the benefits of exploring each option?
- Who can help us with these explorations?
- What are the criteria needed to make the best decisions now?
- What would it look like to follow through on each option?

N egotiating next steps from previous conversations
- How can we move on now?
- How would you summarize where we are now?
- What are the next steps needed?
- Who can help with taking the next steps?
- What is the best time line for us?
- What are the consequences of not moving forward now?

Y es voices frame the next steps
- What have we decided?
- How would you summarize what we have heard from others?
- What is needed now?
- How does what we have heard inform our future?
- How can we celebrate our consensus?

Toolkit for Soulful Leaders and Soulful Organizations
Reference Guide

Refer to www.soulful-leadership.com and the *Guidebook for Soulful Leaders & Organizations: A Coach Approach to Change* by Edward Hammett and James Pierce for additional tools and resources.

Additional Coaching Sources

Compiled by Eddie Hammett, Senior Coach
www.valwoodcoaching.com; www.soulful-leadership.com

Books

Creswell, Jane. *Benefits of Christian Coaching for Ministry Leaders*. St. Louis: Chalice Press, 2006.

———. *Coaching for Excellence*. New York: Penguin Press, 2008.

Ellis, Dave. *Life Coaching: A Manual for Helping Professionals*. Williston, Vt.: Crown House, 2006.

Flaherty, James. *Coaching: Evoking Excellence in Others*. Boston: Butterworth Heinemann, 1999.

Gangel, Kenneth. *Coaching Ministry Teams: Leadership and Management in Christian Organizations*. Eugene, Oreg.: Wipf & Stock, 2005.

Hall, Chad, Bill Copper, and Kathryn McElveen. *Faith Coaching: A Conversational Approach to Helping Others Move Forward in Faith*. Coach Approach Ministries, 2009.

Hammett, Edward. "Discipling Functions of Christian Coaching: The Impact of Coaching on Leaders," 2008 , www.amazonshorts.com.

———. *Spiritual Leadership in a Secular Age: Building Bridges Instead of Barriers*. St. Louis: Chalice Press, 2005.

Hargrove, Robert. *Masterful Coaching*. San Francisco: John Wiley and Sons, 2003.

Hayden, C.J. *Get Clients Now: A 28 Day Marketing Program for Professionals and Consultants*. New York: AMACOM, 1999. www.amacombooks.com

Homan, Madeleine, and Linda Miller, *Coaching in Organizations: Best Coaching Practices from the Ken Blanchard Companies*. San Francisco: Ken Blanchard Companies, 2008.

Jones, Laurie Beth. *Jesus as Life Coach: Learn from the Best*. Nashville: Thomas Nelson, 2004.

Logan, Robert, Sherilyn Carlton, and Tara Miller. *Coaching 101: Discover the Power of Coaching*. Saint Charles, Ill.: Churchsmart Resources, 2003. www.churchsmart.com

Logan, Robert, and Gary Reinecke. *Developing Coaching Excellence*. Five assessment methods to determine your coaching effectiveness along with a step-by-step process to help you identify actions steps. www.churchsmart.com

Marshall, Edward M. *Building Trust at the Speed of Change: The Power of the Relationship-Based Corporation*. New York: AMACOM, 2000.

Miller, Linda, and Chad Hall. *Coaching for Christian Leaders: A Practical Guide*. St. Louis: Chalice Press, 2007.

Nelson, Alan. *Coached by Jesus: 31 Life Changing Questions by the Master*. West Monroe, La.: Howard Publishing, 2005.

Ogne, Steve, and Tim Rohel. *Transformissional Coaching: Empowering Leaders in a Changing Ministry World*. Nashville: B & H Publishing Group, 2008.

Stoltzfus, Tony. *Coaching Questions: A Coach's Guide to Powerful Asking Skills*. New York: Pegasus Creative Arts, 2008.

———. *Leadership Coaching: The Disciplines, Skills and Heart of a Coach*. Booksurge, 2005.

Ting, Sharon, and Peter Scisco. *CCL Handbook of Coaching: A Guide for the Leader Coach*. Center for Creative Leadership. San Francisco: Jossey-Bass, 2006.

Umidi, Joseph. *Transformational Coaching: Bridge Building That Impacts*. Fairfax, Va.: Xulon Press, 2005.

Whitworth, Laura, Henry Kinsey-House, and Phil Sandahl. *Co-Active Coaching: New Skills for Coaching People Toward Success in Work and Life.* Lanham, Md.: Davies-Black, 1998.

Professional Coaching Models, Services, and Training

www.ca-ministries.com—Coach Approach Ministries

www.thecolumbiapartnership.org—The Columbia Partnership

www.coaching.com—Ken Blanchard's organization

www.coachfederation.com—International Coaching Federation

www.coachu.com—Coaching University

www.lifetogether.com—Brett Eastman's model of coaching for small groups

www.churchsmart.com—Robert Logan's model and resources

www.transformationalcoaching.com—through Regent University, Joseph Umidi's ministry

www.churchcoaching.com—John Laster's ministry

www.lifecoachtraining.com—Pat Williams' coaching organization

www.leadfirst.com—Charlotte, N.C., based consulting and coaching services

http://www.cnn.com/2007/LIVING/worklife/08/01/wlb.life.coaches/—article on life coaching and the coaching profession, August 2, 2007

Coaching Tools/Resources/Training

Master's Level Coach Training—Eight different courses designed by Linda Miller, master certified coach, and Jane Creswell, master certified coach. Taught by Coach Approach Ministries, www.ca-ministries.com, as part of certification and degree program at Western Seminary, Portland, Oregon. Satisfies all the required classroom hours for professional certified coach certification through the International Coaching Federation.

Eight Courses include:
1. Building Blocks of Powerful Coaching
2. Establishing a Dynamic Coaching Relationship
3. Change, Transition, and Transformation
4. Coaching as a Learning Catalyst
5. The Language of Coaching
6. Personal Coaching
7. Coaching Teams
8. A Coach Approach to Evangelism and Discipleship

Doctor of Ministry Degree in Christian Coaching—began Fall 2008 through Golden Gate Theological Seminary. See http://www.ggbts.edu/news.aspx?item=15 for more details.

Fast Track Coach Training—replication of the eight courses taught at Western. Taught by Coach Approach Ministries at Hollifield Leadership Center and various other places across the country—see www.hollifield.org. Satisfies classroom hours for a professional certified coach through International Coaching Federation.

NEW Journal of Christian Coaching—www.journalofchristiancoaching.com

Valwood Christian Coaching, www.valwoodcoaching.com, offers Valwood Certification for Christian Coaching. This includes an online introduction, face-to-face foundation class, mentor coaching, and congregational coach training at Hollifield and various other places across the country. Satisfies classroom requirements for associate level of International Coaching Federation.

Links*

"Speed Coaching for Your Career" http://www.nydailynews.com/ money/2008/07/20/2008–07–20_speed_coaching_for_your_career.html

"The Secret Coach" http://money.cnn.com/2008/07/21/technology/reingold_coach. fortune/

"Coaching: A Christian Overview and Response" by Gary Collins http://www. garyrcollins.com/index.php?option=com_content&task=view&id=10&Itemid=8

"Workplace Coaching: Gauging the Impact of a Negative Boss" http://seattlepi. nwsource.com/business/322889_workcoach09.html

"The Wisdom of Coaching " by Peter Webb http://www.intentional.com.au/docs/ tl_book_vol_2_final_peter.pdf

The Philosophy and Practice of Coaching: Insights and Issues for a New Generation http://www.intentional.com.au/ppc_book.html

"Coaching for Wisdom," PowerPoint presentation by Peter Webb http://www. intentional.com.au/docs/17_Webb_2007.pdf

"Develop leaders Through Coaching" http://www.sbpost.ie/post/pages/p/story.aspx-qqqt=People+In+Business-qqqm=nav-qqqid=34821–qqqx=1.asp

"Personal Coaching Helps Clients Soar" http://www.novatoadvance.com/ articles/2008/08/06/business/doc4899fb98e67a8682849586.txt

"Just Coach It Begins Speed Coaching for Executives"

http://www.prweb.com/releases/2008/08/prweb1183354.htm

Prepared by Eddie Hammett, www.thecolumbiapartnership.org; www.ca-ministries.com; www.valwoodcoaching.com; and www.transformingsolutions

* See the *Making Shifts without Making Waves* page on www.chalicepress.com for links to the online sources

Possible Coaching Questions for Making Shifts without Making Waves

Coaching Questions to Consider:

- What emotions scare you?
- What emotions do you feel that you cannot label?
- What have you been looking for in life but have not found?
- What are your pursuits now?
- What would be the impact of living life as not to have "bad experiences"?
- How would you grow a soul that radiates health?
- What is the best expression of your faith in your work?
- What is your typical reaction/behavior when you are sad or angry? Does this at times feel out of control?
- Do you hide things from others and often lie to yourself and others? How would you describe this behavior—healthy or unhealthy?
- How can you become more honest as you begin to step out of denial and strengthen your true self?
- What habit changes would improve your life? Which ones are you willing to change now?
- What old tapes play over and over in your mind that sabotage your future and keep you stuck?
- What new tapes can start playing over your old tapes to propel you forward to health and wholeness?
- Are you a person who always needs to be right?
- Does it upset you to compromise?
- What could help you begin to see things through different lenses if needed?
- Are you willing to change to move toward happiness?
- What is really going on?
- What are the pinches here?
- What are the resources needed to move forward?

Coaching Models for Soulful Leaders
From Pain to Purpose
From Stuck to Unstuck
From Wandering to Walking
From Success to Significance
From Maintenance to Mission to Capacity Building

B ullet-proof

A voidance

R esistance

R oadblocks

I mpulse

E go

R esentment

S abotage

Coaching Models for Soulful Leaders

From Pain to Purpose
From Stuck to Unstuck
From Wandering to Walking
From Success to Significance
From Maintenance to Mission to Capacity Building

B elief Systems

R elationships

I ntention

D iscover

G ifts

E ngagement

S ummarize

www.soulful-leadership.com

Basic Coaching Model

F ocus

A ction

S ummary

T racking

Basic Coaching Skills

L isten

E ncourage

A sk powerful questions

R espond

N egotiate action

Coaching to FACE Change

F ear

A cceptance

C ommunity

E valuation/Exploration

Coaching to MAKE Change

M ovement

A djustment

K inesis

E volution

Coaching to EMBRACE Change

E xperiment

M anage/Maintain

B uild bridges, not Barriers

R ebuild

A lign

C hallenge

E xplode

Revolutionary Transformation = Change + Transition

Notes

Preface

[1]Barack Obama, "Remarks of President-Elect Barack Obama: Election Night," in Chicago, Nov. 4, 2008. Text can be found at http://www.barackobama.com/2008/11/04/remarks_of_presidentelect_bara.php, Video can be found at http://www.youtube.com/watch?v=HfHbw3n0EIM&.

[2]Ken Blanchard and Phil Hodges, *The Most Loving Place in Town* (Nashville: Thomas Nelson, 2008), 123–24.

[3]John Trent, *HeartShifts: The Two Degree Difference that Will Change Your Heart, Your Home and Your Health* (Nashville: Broadman and Holman, 2004), 91–99.

Introduction

[1]Patricia Aburdene, *Megatrends 2010: The Rise of Conscious Capitalism* (Charlottesville, Va.: Hampton Roads Publishing, 2005), xxi.

[2]Anders Gronstedt, "All Aboard! The Web 3D Train is Leaving the Station," *T & D Magazine* (December 2008): 22–26, www.astd.org.

Chapter 1: Making Shifts Without Making Waves—Is It Really Possible?

[1]Leonard Sweet, cited in *Don Everts and Doug Schaupp, I Once Was Lost: What Postmodern Skeptics Taught Us about Their Path to Jesus* (Downers Grove, Ill.: InterVarsity Press, 2008), xi.

[2]Leonard Sweet, *The Church of the Perfect Storm* (Nashville: Abingdon Press, 2008), 11.

[3]Ibid., 5.

[4]Patricia Aburdene, *Megatrends 2010: The Rise of Conscious Capitalism* (Charlottesville, Va.: Hampton Roads Publishing, 2005), 2.

Chapter 2: Soulful Leadership Creates Transformation through Coaching

[1]Richard Florida, *The Flight of the Creative Class: The New Global Competition for Talent* (New York: HarperCollins, 2007), and *The Rise of the Creative Class and How It's Transforming Work, Leisure and Everyday Life* (New York: Perseus Books, 2004).

[2]Leonard Sweet, *The Church of the Perfect Storm* (Nashville: Abingdon Press, 2008), 2.

[3]Ibid., 5.

[4]Ibid., 4.

[5]Colin Morris, *Things Shaken—Things Unshaken: Reflections on Faith and Terror* (London: Epworth Press, 2006), 156, quoted in Ibid., 5.

[6]Sweet, *The Church of the Perfect Storm*, 5.

[7]For more on the subject, see Andrea Buchanan, *Note to Self* (New York: Simon Spotlight Entertainment, 2009).

[8]Jane Creswell, *The Complete Idiot's Guide to Coaching for Excellence* (New York: Alpha Books/Penguin, 2008), 49.

[9]Ibid., 56–59.

[10]Ibid.

[11]Ibid., 3.

Chapter 3: Soulful Leaders Create Harmony through Coaching

[1]From Jim Collins, *Good to Great* (New York: Random House, 2001), 55f. Adapted by Hammett and Pierce

[2]William Bridges, *Transitions: Making Sense of Life's Changes* (Reading, Mass.: Perseus Books, 1980), 112.

[3]Ibid.

[4]Ruth Haley Barton, *Strengthening the Soul of Your Leadership: Seeking God in the Crucible of Ministry* (Downers Grove, Ill.: IVP Books, 2008), 23.

[5]Ibid., 25–27.

[6]Peter M. Senge, *The Fifth Discipline* (New York: Random House, 2006), 26.

[7]James Flaherty, *Coaching: Evoking Excellence in Others* (Boston: Butterworth Heinemann, 1999), 3.

[8]Ibid., 3–4.

[9]Iyanla Vanzant, *In the Meantime* (New York, Simon & Schuster, 1998), 254–55.

[10]John Trent, *HeartShifts: The Two Degree Difference that Will Change Your Heart, Your Home and Your Health* (Nashville: Broadman and Holman, 2004), 22.

[11]Collins, *Good to Great*, 13.

[12]Chad Hall, Bill Copper, and Kathryn McElveen, *FaithCoaching: A Conversational Approach to Helping Others Move Forward in Faith* (Coach Approach Ministries, 2009).

Chapter 4: Soulful Leaders Put Heart into Managing Chanage

[1]James Morrison, "How to Manage a Crisis," *The Independent* (London), Jan. 22, 2009, http://www.independent.co.uk/student/postgraduate/postgraduate-study/how-to-manage-a-crisis-1479583.html.

[2]Acronym developed by Suzanne Goebel, PCC (www.theonpurposecompany.com), Jane Creswell, MCC (www.internal-impact.com), and Linda Miller, MCC (www.ca-ministries.com). Used by written permission. Compare Linda J. Miller and Chad W. Hall, *Coaching for Christian Leaders: A Practical Guide* (St. Louis: Chalice Press, 2007) and Jane Creswell, *Christ-Centered Coaching: 7 Benefits for Ministry Leaders* (St. Louis: Chalice Press, 2006).

[3]Framed and developed by Suzanne Goebel—www.theonpurposecompany.com.

[4]Jim Collins, *Good to Great* (New York: Random House, 2001), 98.

[5]Adapted by Edward Hammett from Michael Frost and Alan Hirsch, *The Shaping of Things to Come: Innovation and Mission for the 21st Century Church* (Peabody, Mass.: Hendrickson, 2003).

[6]Jim Collins, *How the Mighty Fall: And Why Some Companies Never Give In* (New York: Random House, 2009).

[7]For more information on this subject, see William Bridges, *Managing Transitions* (New York: Da Capo Press, 2003, 2nd ed.).

Chapter 5: Making Shifts That Matter in Individuals

[1]Jane Creswell, *The Complete Idiot's Guide to Coaching for Excellence* (New York: Alpha Books, 2008), 44.

[2]William Bridges, *Managing Transitions* (New York: Da Capo Press, 2003, 2d ed.), 8.

[3]Ibid., 119, emphasis added.

[4]Ibid.

[5]Ibid., 120.

[6]Iyanla Vanzant, *In the Meantime* (New York, Simon & Schuster, 1998), 52.

[7]W. Timothy Gallwey, *The Inner Game of Work* (New York: Random House, 2001), 28.

[8]Dictionary.com, s.v. "impulse," http://dictionary.reference.com/browse/impulse (accessed Feb. 26, 2009).

[9]Wayne Dyer, *The Power of Intention* (Carlsbad, Calif.: Hay House, 2004), 233.

[10]Ibid., 233ff.

[11]Terence T. Gorski, *Getting Love Right, Learning the Choices of Healthy Intimacy* (New York: Simon and Schuster, 1993), 33–35.

[12]Creswell, *Idiot's Guide*, 102–4.

[13]Ingrid Bacci, as quoted at www.thedailyguru.com, "The Daily Guru," spiritual messages.

[14]Gary Zukav, *The Seat of the Soul* (New York: Simon and Schuster, 1990), 247.

Chapter 6: Making Shifts That Matter in Institutions/Organizations

[1]Patrick Lencioni, *Five Dysfunctions of a Team* (San Francisco: Jossey Bass, 2002), 188–93.

[2]Ibid., 197–220.

[3]Ibid.,191–93.

[4]Patrick Lencioni offers excellent tools for working with teams in *The Five Dysfunctions of a Team*. Jane Creswell offers some practical summary statements to guide the coach in working with dysfunctional teams, Jane Creswell, *The Complete Idiot's Guide to Coaching for Excellence* (New York: Alpha Books, 2008), 44.

[5]Creswell, *Idiot's Guide*, 103.

[6]Everett Rogers, *Diffusion of Innovations*, 4th ed. (New York: Free Press, 1995); Malcolm Gladwell, *The Tipping Point: How Little Things Can Make a Big Difference* (Boston: Back Bay Books, 2002).

[7]Natalie Gillam, "Be a Successful Business Leader Even in Tough Times," *Emirates Business* 24/7, Nov. 28, 2008, http://www.business24–7.ae/Articles/2008/11/Pages/11282008_64e116def112417da687f13107b9715d.aspx

[8]Ibid.

[9]Keith M. Eades, *The New Solution Selling* (New York: McGraw-Hill, 2004), 244.

[10]Ibid., 256.

[11]Much of the material in this chapter is from Craig Dowden, "Spotlight on Coaching as a Leadership Development Activity—Some Issues to Consider," *Ottawa Business Journal* (Nov. 28, 2008), accessed through ottawabusinessjournal.com.

[12]Ibid.

[13]Holly B. Tompson, Mark Vickers, Institute for Corporate Productivity, Judy London, Carol L. Morrison, "Coaching: A Global Study of Successful Practices," American Management Association paper, 24. See http://www.amanet.org.

[14]Dowden, "Spotlight."

Chapter 7: Sustaining Soulful Leadership

[1]Brian D. McLaren, "We Are in Deep Shift," http://deepshift.org/site/?p=16, used with permission of Brian McLaren.

[2]See Annette Simmons at www.groupprocessingconsulting.com—*Whoever Tells the Best Story Wins* (New York: Amacom Book Division, 2007); *The Story Factor: Inspiration, Influence, and Persuasion Through the Art of Storytelling*, rev. ed. (New York: Perseus Books, 2006); *Territorial Games: Understanding and Ending Turf Wars at Work* (New York: Amacom, 1997); and *Safe Place for Dangerous Truths* (New York: Amacom, 2006) are some of her newest books.

[3]"The Six Stories You Need to Know How to Tell," International Storytelling Center, excerpted from Annette Simmons, *The Story Factor*, http://www.storytellingcenter.com/resources/articles/simmons.htm.

BOOKS BY
The Columbia Partnership Ministry Partners

George W. Bullard Jr.
Every Congregation Needs a Little Conflict
Pursuing the Full Kingdom Potential of Your Congregation

Richard L. Hamm
Recreating the Church

Edward H. Hammett
Reaching People under 40 while Keeping People over 60:
Being Church to All Generations

Spiritual Leadership in a Secular Age:
Building Bridges Instead of Barriers

A full listing and description of TCP resources is available at
www.chalicepress.com and
www.thecolumbiapartnership.org